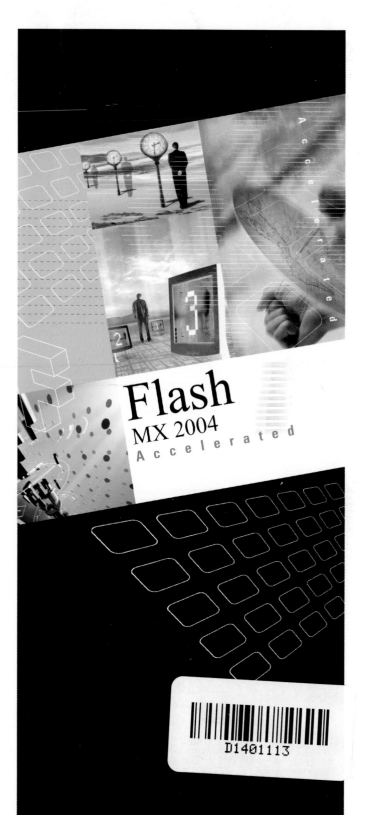

Flash
MX 2004
Accelerated

Y.

Manager: **Suzie Lee**
Chief Editor: **Angelica Lim**
Developmental Editor: **Colleen Wheeler Strand**
Production Editor: **Patrick Cunningham**
Editor: **Sas Jacobs**
Proofreader: **Semtle**
Cover Designer: **Changwook Lee**
Book Designer: **Litmus**
Production Control: **Ann Lee**
Indexer: **Katrine Poon**

ISBN: 89-314-3506-1

Printed and bound in the Republic of Korea.

**How to contact us**

E-mail: support@youngjin.com
feedback@youngjin.com.sg
Address: YoungJin.com
1623-10, Seocho-dong, Seocho-gu, Seoul 137-878, Korea
Telephone: +65-6327-1161
Fax: +65-6327-1151

# Flash

## MX 2004

Accelerated

YJ IT Publishing Team

contents

**Chapter** | 1

# Exploring the Flash MX 2004 Workspace

This first chapter is a warm-up to prepare you for your Flash MX 2004 adventure. It provides a quick introduction to Flash, and is a valuable resource for beginners who want to learn the basics quickly so they can proceed with the hands-on exercises in this book. For designers and developers with experience in previous versions of Flash, there's a section on the new features in Flash MX 2004 so you can get up to speed in no time.

# The Flash MX 2004 Interface

Macromedia Flash is an important software tool for creating multimedia content. It has grown from a simple animation package into a powerful tool that can be used to build software applications. The latest edition of Flash comes as part of the Macromedia Studio MX 2004 family and provides more user-friendly features and a wider range of functionalities than earlier releases.

## The 10 New Features of Flash MX 2004

### 1. Start Page

The start page appears each time you open Flash MX 2004 and whenever there are no open Flash movie files. It provides a quick way to open recent files or to create new Flash movies. You can also use the start page to create a Flash file based on a template.

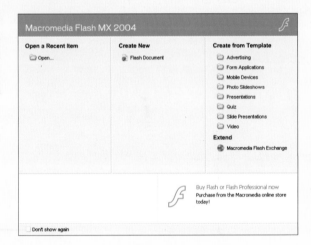

### 2. Timeline Effects

Timeline effects is a new feature that allows you to add animation effects in a single step. You can add a blur or drop shadow; duplicate an object; or transform an object's color, position, or rotation in a fraction of the time it would have taken you with earlier versions of Flash. Timeline effects can be edited or removed at any time, making them one of the most useful new features in Flash MX 2004.

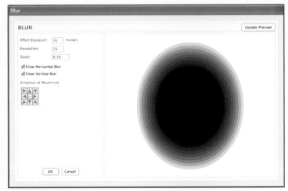

Applying the Blur Effect

Applying the Distributed Duplicate Effect          Applying the Explode Effect

## 3. Video Import Wizard

Flash MX 2004 makes it easier to import video clips by using the Video Import wizard. The wizard can perform simple video editing tasks and adjust settings such as compression, cropping, and scaling.

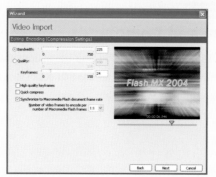

## 4. Text Features

Flash MX 2004 includes new text features such as support for Cascading Style Sheets (CSS), a spellchecker, and a global search-and-replace. You can also add vertical and horizontal text scrolling and text optimization features to prevent your text from being illegible at small sizes and low resolutions.

By supporting CSS, Flash MX 2004 allows you to use the same text styles in HTML pages and Flash movies.

```
A:link     {font-family:arial,helvetica;
            font-size:12px
            text-decoration: none;
            color: 000000;}
A:active   {font-family:arial,helvetica;
            text-decoration: underline;
            color: F64304;}2
A:visited  {font-family:arial,helvetica;
            text-decoration: none;
            color: #0347AD;}
A:hover    {font-family:arial,helvetica;
            text-decoration: underline;
            color: F64304;}
```

## 5. Improved Drawing Tools

Flash MX 2004 includes the new PolyStar and Free Transform tools.

### PolyStar Tool ()

The PolyStar tool is used to draw multi-sided shapes such as polygons and stars. You can easily change the shape options using the Tool Settings dialog box.

### Free Transform Tool (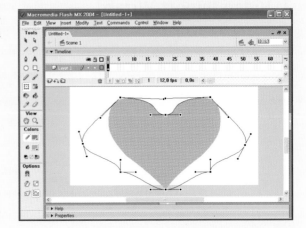)

The Free Transform tool allows you to position, scale, rotate, skew, and distort an object with a single tool.

## 6. History Panel and Commands

The History panel within Flash MX 2004 shows all the actions that you've carried out in the current session, step by step. You can use this panel to return to a specific point in your editing or to automate your actions.

## 7. Behaviors Panel

The Behaviors panel allows designers to add actions within their movies without having to learn programming. Behaviors can control objects such as movie clips, navigation elements, sound, and video and will be familiar to users of Dreamweaver.

## 8. Components Panel and the Component Inspector

Flash MX 2004 includes a set of user interface components such as buttons, combo boxes, radio buttons, and text input fields that can be used to build forms. These components can be dragged onto the stage and easily edited using the Component Inspector.

## 9. Help Panel

Help information in Flash MX 2004 is no longer viewed within a Web browser. The new Help panel contains reference materials and tutorials, and displays in a separate panel. In addition, help content can be automatically updated from the Macromedia Web site.

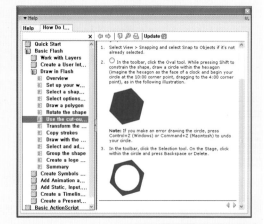

## 10. Macromedia Flash Player 7

Flash MX 2004 includes Flash Player 7 to play SWF files. This version of the player improves movie performance compared with earlier versions and includes faster graphics display and video playback—as well as better memory usage.

Flash is a very versatile software package that offers many benefits to both designers and programmers. This section lists some of the advantages of using Flash in your work.

- Flash mainly uses vector graphics, allowing for small file sizes and high quality images.
- The Flash Player plug-in is widely distributed, which makes it possible to watch Flash movies from just about any computer.
- Flash MX 2004 has a user-friendly interface aimed at both designers and programmers.
- Flash MX 2004 supports streaming technology so that movies can be viewed as they are being downloaded. Streaming can speed up the process when viewing very large movies.
- Flash MX 2004 allows you to include content from databases and XML files in your movies.

## Creative Uses for Flash

There are many creative uses for Flash MX 2004, including:
- Cartoon animations
- Web sites
- Flash games
- Flash cards
- Flash forums
- Internet advertisements

In addition, devices other than computers, such as cell phones and PDAs, can play Flash movies. This section aims to provide an overview of some of the creative work that can be done with Flash.

### Cartoon Animation

From the very beginning, Flash has been used as an animation tool for drawing and animating 2D cartoons. The Internet has introduced an incredible variety of new cartoon characters to a wide audience, and has increased the popularity of cartoons worldwide.

http://www.hatoo.net

http://woobiboy.intz.com

## Web Sites

When Flash was first introduced, it was used mainly for enhancing Web sites, often with small animations or introduction movies. More recently, entire Web sites have been contained in a single Flash movie, and examples often feature clever multimedia and a high degree of user interactivity.

## Flash Games

As Flash evolved, programmers were able to create movies that contain complex programming instructions written in ActionScript. One of the most common uses for ActionScript has been in creating multimedia games. One advantage of using Flash for creating games is that game file sizes can remain small while still containing exciting sound and visual effects. Flash games can also be played directly from the Web browser.

http://www.tvo.org

## Flash Cards

Electronic postcards have been popular on the Internet for some time. Flash has allowed e-cards to include animations, sound, and even video. E-cards created in Flash can also include user interactivity for a more personal experience.

## Flash Forums

Flash forums allow more interesting interfaces or skins than their HTML-based counterparts. There are many Flash forum services available on the Internet today.

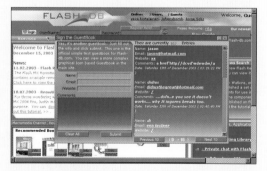

http://www.flash-db.com

## Internet Advertisements

Flash movies have been a popular means of advertising on the Internet, as they are more flexible then their animated GIF counterparts. Flash ads can include multimedia and user interaction with relatively small file sizes. Some flash advertisements are so complex that it can seem like you're watching a commercial on television.

# Installing Flash MX 2004

This section provides information about installing and using Flash MX 2004. Instructions for downloading and installing Macromedia's 30-day trial version of Flash MX 2004 are also included.

## Downloading a Trial Version

If you do not have a copy of the latest Flash MX 2004, you can download a 30-day trial copy from the Macromedia Web site.

1 Start Internet Explorer. Type in http://www.macromedia.com/ in the address field and hit [Enter]. From the menu at the top of the Web page, choose [Downloads] - [Free Trials].

2 Find Flash MX 2004 in the product list and click on [Try].

tip >>

**If You Do Not Have a Password**

If you don't have a Macromedia password, select No, I will Create One Now and then click [Continue]. Type in the relevant information on the password setup page and then click [Continue].

3 In the Register and Download window, type in your e-mail address and your Macromedia password (if you have one) and click [Continue].

4 In the Macromedia Trial Downloads page, you can download the trial program in the language and the operating system of your choice. In the Flash MX 2004 & Flash MX Professional 2004 drop-down menu, choose English | Windows | 76.02MB.

5 After selecting the system requirements for Flash MX 2004 & Flash MX Professional 2004, click on [Download]. When the File Download dialog box appears, click [Save].

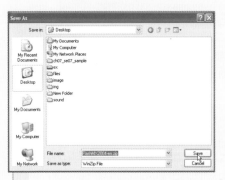

6 In the Save As dialog box, choose the folder where you wish to save the trial program and then click [Save].

7 Your download will begin automatically.

1 | Double-click the **Install_Flash_MX_2004.exe** file to start the installation. You should see the dialog box pictured above.

2 | When you see the above dialog box, click [Next] to continue.

3 | Before you can install the file, you will be asked to accept the license agreement. Click the [Yes] button to accept the agreement and carry on with the installation. If you click [No], the installation will end.

4 | In this step, you will decide where to install the program. Click [Next] to install Flash in the Programs folder, or use the [Browse] button to choose a different location.

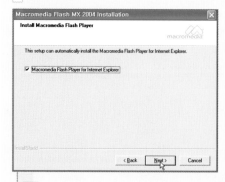

5 | You will then be asked if you would like to install Flash Player. This is generally advisable and you should leave the box checked. Click [Next] to continue.

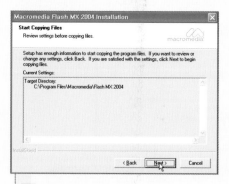

6 | Click [Next] to begin installing or click [Back] to change your settings. You will need to go back to change the target drive if it does not have enough disk space.

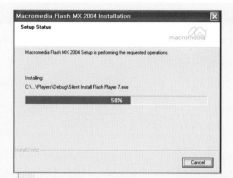

7 Once you've clicked [Next] the installation will begin.

8 When the installation has finished, you will see a message stating that the installation is complete. Click the [Finish] button to close the dialog box.

tip >>

## Installing in Microsoft Windows 98 or 2000

When installing Flash MX 2004 on Windows 98 or 2000, you will see a message that tells you to restart your computer after the installation is complete. Click [Finish] to end the installation and reboot your computer. You must reboot the computer in order for Flash to work properly.

# Starting and Quitting Flash MX 2004

This section covers how to start Flash MX 2004 and how to close it down when you've finished. Throughout the rest of the book, we will use the terms movie, file, and document to refer to a Flash file.

## Starting Flash

1 To start Flash, navigate to [Start] - [Program] - [Macromedia] - [Macromedia Flash MX 2004] using the [Start] button at the bottom-left area of the screen. Click [Macromedia Flash MX 2004].

2 Open the trial software by clicking the, "I want to try Macromedia Flash," option and press [Continue].

tip >>
### Switching Versions

When evaluating the trial edition of Flash MX 2004, you can switch between the Standard and Professional versions at any time. When you purchase the software, you can only buy a single version and you won't be able to switch to the other version.

3 The next dialog box asks you which version of Flash you would like to try. The Standard version is aimed at designers, while the Professional version is aimed at programmers. Choose the "Flash MX 2004" option and click [OK].

4 You will be asked whether you would like to download new help contents. Click [Yes] to update the help contents using an Internet connection.

5 Flash MX 2004 will start and the start page will appear. Click the, "Create New Flash Document," link in the middle of the page to start working on a new movie.

## Shutting Down Flash

1 To exit Flash, select [File] - [Exit] from the menu bar at the top.

tip >>

### Creating a Flash Shortcut on the Desktop

- If you have any unsaved documents you will be prompted to save them before Flash closes down. If you are prompted this time, click [No], as you won' t have any work that needs to be saved. The next chapter will discuss how to save your work in more detail.

- If you are going to use Flash frequently, it may be useful to create a shortcut icon on your desktop so you don' t have to search through the All Programs list each time you want to use Flash. You can do this by locating the Flash program, [Start] - [Program] - [Macromedia] - [Macromedia Flash MX 2004], and right-clicking on it. A shortcut menu will appear and you should click on [Send To] - [Desktop (create shortcut)].

When you view the desktop, you should see a shortcut icon. Double-click the icon to start Flash MX 2004.

Flash 2004 Shortcut Icon on the Desktop

The first part of this chapter covered installing, starting, and closing Flash. In this section, we will look at some of the features of Flash and show you how you can use them.

## The New Flash MX 2004 Start Page

The start page is new to Flash MX 2004. It appears when you first open Flash and whenever there are no movies open. The start page shows a list of your recent files and allows you to create a new movie. It also shows the different templates that are available within Flash.

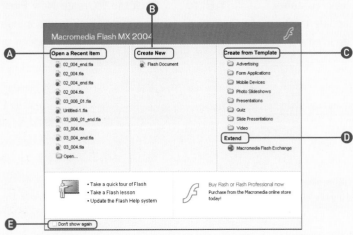

Start Page with Lists

### Ⓐ Open a Recent Item

This section lists movies that you have worked on recently. You can browse for more files by clicking on the [Open] icon.

### Ⓑ Create New

The [Create New] - [Flash Document] option creates a new blank Flash movie.

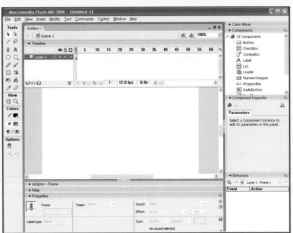

A New Movie Created by Clicking
[Create New] - [Flash Document]

### ⊙ Create from Template

This section lists the standard templates available within Flash. Click a category to see the available templates. You can use these templates to create a new Flash movie.

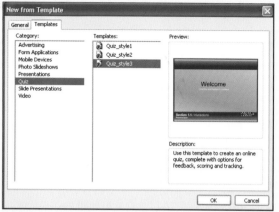

Selecting a Template

### ⊙ Extend

The [Extend] - [Macromedia Flash Exchange] option links to the Macromedia Web site where you can download extras for Flash such as components.

Clicking on [Extend] - [Macromedia Flash Exchange] to Connect to the Macromedia Web site

### ⊙ Don't Show Again

This option allows you to stop the start page from appearing in the future.

## Screen Elements

When you first see the Flash MX 2004 workspace, it can look a little daunting. The aim of this part of the book is to familiarize you with the different elements of the screen.

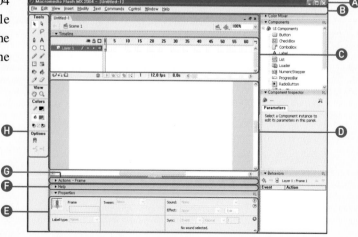

### Ⓐ Title Bar

The title bar displays the name of the current movie and the software.

### Ⓑ Menu Bar

The menu bar provides one way to control Flash. The menu bar is organized into sections. Some of the included commands are available in other parts of Flash.

### Ⓒ Timeline

The timeline shows the structure of the Flash movie. It is used to create and edit the timing of animations.

### Ⓓ Stage

One way to understand Flash is to treat each movie as a play, made up of objects and text (actors) appearing on a stage. The stage is the location for the objects and text that you want to animate.

### Ⓔ Property Inspector

The Property Inspector shows the properties of whatever object is currently selected. If nothing is selected, the properties of the document are displayed.

### Ⓕ Help

The Help panel shows help topics, reference materials, and a "How Do I" section. The contents can be automatically updated from the Macromedia Web site.

### Ⓖ Actions

The Actions panel shows any ActionScript that has been added to a movie.

### Ⓗ Toolbox

The toolbox contains drawing (and other common) tools needed to create Flash movies.

tip >>

**Other Panels**

Flash contains a number of other panels that provide options for working in Flash. These will be covered in more detail a little later in the chapter.

### A New Document Interface in Flash MX 2004

If you have worked with Macromedia Dreamweaver, the Flash MX 2004 interface will look familiar to you. When you maximize a movie in Flash MX 2004, you will notice that the top of the movie contains a tabbed movie title bar. This can be useful when you are working with multiple movies as it enables you to switch between them easily.

Flash movies can be divided into different scenes, and the top of the movie shows the name of the current scene. It also shows the name of any object that is being edited. This information has been moved from below the timeline where it appeared in earlier versions. The Edit Scene, Edit Symbol, and Zoom options have also been moved to the top of the timeline.

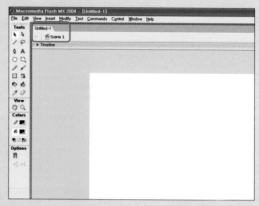

A maximized Flash movie without the timeline and panels.

# The Timeline

The timeline shows the structure of your movie. To continue our play analogy, the timeline shows a diagram of all of the acts in the play, indicating which actors are on the stage and what they are doing.

Learning to use the timeline is an essential part of working with Flash. The timeline includes the frames and layers that make up a Flash movie, and is used constantly when movies are being created and edited. As you click a different part of the timeline, that part of the movie will appear on the stage below.

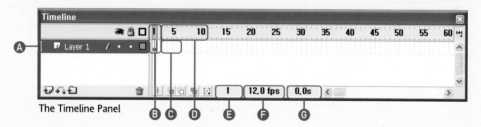

The Timeline Panel

## Ⓐ Layers

Layers will be familiar to people who use Photoshop. They can be thought of as transparent sheets that contain objects and text for your movie. Layers allow you to control the stacking order of objects in the movie.

## Ⓑ Playhead

You can click and drag the playhead along the timeline to select a new frame. The playhead is like a pointer that moves through each frame—in order—when a flash movie is played.

## Ⓒ Frames

Frames are the smallest unit of a movie, and each is numbered starting at 1. All animations are made up of frames played in order. There are different types of frames within Flash; this will be covered in more detail later in the book.

### ⓓ `1  5  10`Timeline Header

The timeline header shows the frame numbers as well as the position of the playhead.

### ⓔ `1` Current Frame Position

This box displays the frame number of the currently selected frame.

### ⓕ `12.0 fps` Elapsed Speed

Each movie has its own frame rate, measured in number of frames per second (fps). The play speed shows how many frames of the movie will be played per second. At 12 fps, 12 frames will take one second to play. The higher the frame rate, the more frames are played each second and the faster the movie will run.

### ⓖ `0.0s` Play Time

The play time shows how much time it will take to play the movie up to the playhead. If the playhead is at the beginning of the movie, the play time will be 0.0s.

## The Toolbox

The toolbox contains all of the drawing tools and other tools that you will need to create movies in Flash. It is a little like Flash's own Swiss Army knife! The toolbox contains a total of 18 different tools that do everything from creating shapes and lines to adding text and even transforming your graphics. Learning to use the tools in the toolbox is an essential part of creating Flash movies.

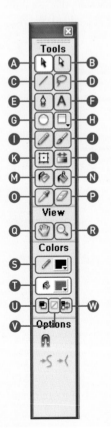

Ⓐ Selection Tool - The arrow is called the Selection tool and is used to select and move objects within your movies. Pressing [v] on the keyboard brings up this tool.

Ⓑ Subselection Tool - This tool is used to modify the border of an object or change its shape. It can be accessed quickly with the letter [a].

Ⓒ Line Tool - The Line tool is used to draw straight lines and can be used by pressing [n] on the keyboard.

Ⓓ Lasso Tool - This tool is used create selections within a movie. You can use it to draw the area that you would like to select. Press [l] on the keyboard to activate the tool.

Ⓔ Pen Tool - The Pen tool is used for creating paths and will be familiar to users of Photoshop. It creates anchor points that can be used to draw curves or straight lines, and it takes a little practice to get the hang of. Press [p] to use this tool.

Ⓕ Text Tool - The Text tool is used to add text to a movie. Pressing [t] brings up this tool.

Ⓖ Oval Tool - The Oval tool draws oval and circular shapes and can be activated by pressing [o] on the keyboard.

Ⓗ Rectangle Tool - This tool draws square and rectangular shapes. Clicking and holding down the left mouse button on this tool opens a menu that allows you to switch to the PolyStar tool. Both tools can be accessed by pressing the letter [r] on the keyboard.

**I** 🖉 **Pencil Tool** - The Pencil tool is used to draw freeform lines and can be activated by pressing [y] on the keyboard.

**J** 🖌 **Brush Tool** - The Brush tool simulates drawing with a brush. You can vary the size and tip shapes of the brush. This tool is accessed by pressing [b] on the keyboard.

**K** ⊡ **Free Transform Tool** - The Free Transform tool is used to modify properties of graphical objects such as size, rotation, and distortion. It can be activated by pressing [q] on the keyboard.

**L** 🔲 **Fill Transform Tool** - The Fill Transform tool makes changes to the size and direction of an object filled with a gradient. The tool can be activated by pressing [f] on the keyboard.

**M** 🖉 **Ink Bottle Tool** - The Ink Bottle tool can be used to add a border or to change the color of an existing border. Press [s] on the keyboard to use this tool.

**N** 🪣 **Paint Bucket Tool** - The Paint Bucket tool fills objects with color or changes the existing color of objects. This tool can be activated by pressing [k] on the keyboard.

**O** 🖉 **Eyedropper Tool** - The Eyedropper tool samples color and can be accessed by pressing the [i] key.

**P** 🖉 **Eraser Tool** - The Eraser tool can be used in a number of different ways to erase parts of objects. Press the [e] key to activate this tool.

**Q** ✋ **Hand Tool** - The Hand tool is used to drag the stage so that you can see selected parts of your movie. You can hit the [h] key to bring up this tool.

**R** 🔍 **Zoom Tool** - The Zoom tool zooms in or out of the stage. The tool can be accessed by hitting [m] and [z].

**S** 🖉◼ **Line Color Tool** - The Line Color tool allows you to choose the color of a line. This is also referred to as the Stroke Color tool.

**T** 🪣◼ **Fill Color Tool** - The Fill Color tool is used to choose the fill color of an object.

**U** 🔲 **Black and White Button** - This button allows you to return the line and fill colors to their default settings (i.e., the line color is black and the fill color is white).

**V** ◻ **No Color Button** - This button indicates that no color has been selected.

**W** 🔁 **Swap Colors Button** - Clicking this button swaps the selected line and fill colors.

## The Property Inspector

The Property Inspector shows you all of the properties of any object that you select. The properties will change each time you select a new tool in the toolbox or an object on the stage. If nothing is selected, the panel displays the properties of the document.

### No selection

When nothing is selected, the Property Inspector shows document properties including the size of the movie, the background color, and the frame rate.

### Selecting the Text Tool

When the Text tool is selected, the Property Inspector displays text properties such as font, font size, color, and alignment.

### Selecting a Graphical Object

When you select an object that you have drawn in Flash, the Property Inspector displays the height, width, and x and y positions of the object. It also allows you to change the line and fill colors, and line thickness.

### Selecting Frames

When you select frames in the timeline, the Property Inspector shows frame properties. These properties allow you to create animations and insert sounds.

### Selecting Symbols

Graphical objects that you reuse are called symbols. Selecting a symbol displays symbol properties, such as the position of the symbol and type of symbol, in the Property Inspector.

## Other Panels in Flash MX 2004

Flash MX 2004 has introduced a number of new panels including the Help, Behaviors, and History panels. Within the Window menu, panels have been grouped according to their function. Panels are split into design panels, development panels, and other panels.

### Help Panel

The Help panel contains all of the Flash MX 2004 help documentation as well as tutorials and a comprehensive search function. The "How Do I" section provides information about how to carry out specific tasks within Flash. You can also update the contents of the Help panel by downloading the most current help file from the Macromedia Web site.

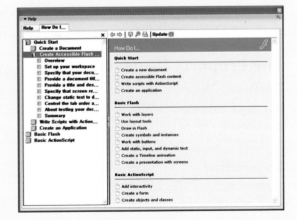

## The Design Panels

There are six design panels that can be opened by choosing [Windows] - [Design Panels]. Click a panel name to open it in the work area. You can also open panels by using their shortcut key.

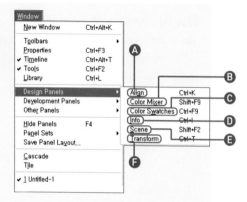

### Ⓐ Align

The Align panel is used to align, arrange, and distribute objects evenly on the stage. The shortcut keys for this panel are [Ctrl]-[K].

### Ⓑ Color Mixer

This panel is used to mix colors that can then be used for lines, fills, gradients, and text. The panel is accessed with the shortcut keys [Shift]-[F9].

### Ⓒ Color Swatches

The Color Swatches panel displays blocks of color that you can use for objects in Flash. You can also use the panel to save and load swatch files. The shortcut keys are [Ctrl]-[F9].

### Ⓓ Info

The Info panel displays information such as object position, size, and color. It can be accessed with the shortcut [Ctrl]-[I].

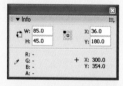

### Ⓔ Scene

As in a play, each movie can be divided into multiple scenes. The Scene panel can be used to add, edit, and delete scenes within your movie. This panel can be displayed using the shortcut [Shift]-[F2].

### Ⓕ Transform

The Transform panel can be used to change the size, rotation, and skew of an object and can be accessed with [Ctrl]-[T].

## The Development Panels

There are six development panels that are listed in [Windows] - [Development Panels]. You can open a panel by clicking its name or by using its shortcut key.

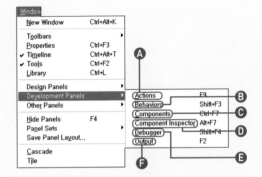

### Ⓐ Actions

The Actions panel is used to add ActionScript to a movie. This panel is used quite extensively by programmers and can be accessed with the [F9] key.

### Ⓑ Behaviors

The Behaviors panel will be familiar to Dreamweaver users. The panel contains a number of actions that can be added to your movie. Behaviors can range from simple actions, such as linking to a Web page or playing a sound, to very complicated actions such as triggering a data source. The panel can be accessed with the shortcut [Shift]-[F3].

### Ⓒ Components

The Components panel contains user interface components that can be used for creating applications. You can also add free and commercial components. The panel is shown using the shortcut [Ctrl]-[F7].

### Ⓓ Component Inspector

The Component Inspector panel shows the properties of components that are on the stage. You can change the properties by clicking the component and making the changes in the Component Inspector. The Component Inspector can be displayed with [Alt]-[F7].

### Ⓔ Debugger

The Debugger panel is used for finding and fixing ActionScript errors. It can be shown with [Shift]-[F4].

### Ⓕ Output

The Output panel is used by programmers to list trace and debugger actions. The window can be displayed with the [F2] key.

## Other Panels

There are five other panels in the [Windows] - [Other Panels] section of the menu. Again, you can click the title or use the shortcut key to open each panel.

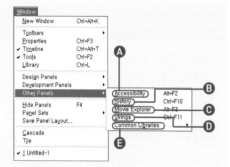

### Ⓐ Accessibility

The Accessibility panel is used to provide text alternatives for Flash movie objects to make them accessible to people with disabilities. The panel uses the [Alt]-[F2] shortcut keys.

### Ⓑ History

The History panel shows a list of all the actions that have been carried out in the current session. The shortcut keys for this panel are [Ctrl]-[F10].

### Ⓒ Movie Explorer

The Movie Explorer shows all of the graphics, objects, and components that have been used within the movie. The Movie Explorer can be accessed with the [Alt]-[F3] shortcut.

### Ⓓ Strings

The Strings panel allows a movie to be published in multiple languages. It uses the [Ctrl]-[F11] shortcut keys.

### Ⓔ Common Libraries

The Common Libraries contain symbols, such as buttons, that come free with Flash MX 2004.

Before you start creating movies, it's important to become comfortable working within the Flash environment and using the Flash tools. Developing these skills will help speed up the process of creating Flash movies. This section explains some of the simple processes that you'll need to use in Flash.

## Basic Movie Setup

Before you start creating your movie, you will need to set up the movie's height and width, background color, and frame rate.

❶ Create a new movie by choosing [File] - [New]. Click on the stage so that the Property Inspector shows the document properties.

❷ You can change the size of the movie by clicking on the [Size] button in the Property Inspector.

❸ You can change other document settings by following the directions below.

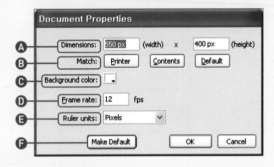

Ⓐ **Dimensions:** Width and height of movie. You can enter your own values for the width and height of the movie.

Ⓑ **Match:** Set the size of the movie to [Printer], [Contents], or [Default]. Clicking these buttons will automatically change the width and height of the movie.

Ⓒ **Background color:** Use the color palette to select a background color for the movie.

Ⓓ **Frame rate:** Set the speed of the movie in frames per second. As this number gets higher, more frames will play in each second of your movie.

Ⓔ **Ruler units:** Set the units used by the ruler. You can choose pixels, points, or centimeters.

Ⓕ **Make Default:** Change all settings back to their default values.

Another way of changing the background color is to click on the Background Color box in the Property Inspector.

**Other Methods**

You can also change document properties by selecting [Modify] - [Document]. (Shortcut keys: [Ctrl]-[J]).

# Working with the Stage

Becoming familiar with the stage is another important step in developing your Flash skills. Some of the more important skills are covered in the next part of this chapter.

## Using the Hand Tool

The Hand tool is used to navigate around your Flash movie and is particularly important when you cannot see all of the stage.

❶ Click [File] - [Open] to open the sample file, **01_001.fla.**

❷ In the toolbox, click the Hand tool in the View section of the toolbox (🖐). The mouse pointer will change to a hand.

❸ Click and hold down the left mouse button on the picture of the cactus. Drag the picture to the left and release the mouse button.

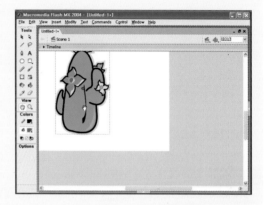

If you are working with another tool and want to switch to the Hand tool, simply hold down the space bar and hold down the left mouse button to move the document on the stage.

## Using the Zoom Tool

❶ Click the Zoom tool in the View section of the toolbox (🔍). The mouse pointer changes to a magnifying glass.

❷ At the bottom of the toolbox, in the Options section, there are two magnifying glasses—one with a plus sign (🔍) and the other with a minus sign (🔍).

❸ The magnifying glass with the plus sign is used to zoom into an area. You can either click on the movie or drag a selection area with the tool.

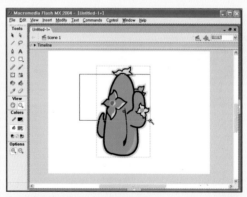

Dragging the Zoom Tool to Select an Area to Magnify

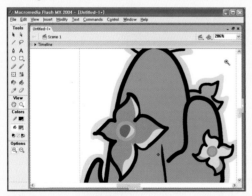

Magnifying the Selected Area

❹ The magnifying glass with the minus sign zooms out. Again, you can click with it or drag a selection area.

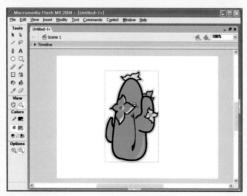

Zooming Out

# Panel Sets

A panel set is a layout for the Flash workspace. Panel sets change the workspace by opening and arranging different panels. Flash MX 2004 ships with two basic panel sets–Default Layout and Training Layout. These sets can be accessed by selecting [Windows] - [Panel Sets] and then choosing either [Default Layout] or [Training Layout].  The Default Layout is used when a new movie is first opened. The Training Layout is useful when learning Flash, because it features a simplified workspace with the Help panel.

You can open and close panels at any time, as well as save your own panel layout.

Default Layout

Training Layout

# The Panels Window

Learning how to work with panels in Flash is very important. Opening the right panels can let you work more efficiently on your movies. However, there are a large number of panels so it is important to strike a balance between opening the panels you need and keeping your workspace uncluttered.  This section looks at how to work with panels more efficiently.

## Minimizing Panels

You can minimize a panel to reduce the amount of space it takes up on the screen. Minimize it by clicking on the down arrow at the left of the panel title bar. It will change to a right-pointing arrow.

## Maximizing Panels

When a panel is minimized, you can reveal it by clicking on the right-pointing arrow at the left of the panel title bar. It will change to a down-pointing arrow.

## Closing Panels

To close a panel, right-click the mouse on the panel title bar and select [Close Panel].

## Viewing the Panel Options Menu

Click on the [Panel Options] button to show the options menu.

## Hiding All Panels

You can hide all panels by pressing the [F4] key or by choosing [Windows] - [Hide Panels]. The panels won't close, but they will be temporarily hidden. If there is a checkmark next to the [Hide Panels] menu, the panels are already hidden. Click the [Hide Panels] option or press the [F4] key to view the panels again. The [F4] key works as a toggle to hide and show panels.

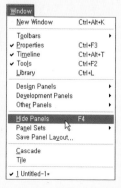

### Minimizing All Vertical and Horizontal Panels

If you need to create some more workspace, you can minimize all the horizontal and vertical panel spaces at the right and bottom of the screen. Click on the arrow button in the center of the vertical panel space to move all panels to the right. When the panels are hidden, you can click this button again to restore the panels to their original positions. The horizontal panel space also has a central arrow button that hides the panels at the bottom of the screen. Again, once hidden, you can click the button to move the panels back to their original positions.

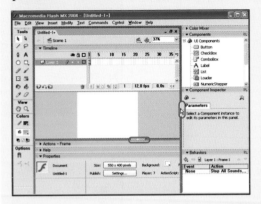 

tip >>

To create a larger workspace, you can also minimize the Timeline panel by clicking the down arrow to the left of the timeline title bar. Click the arrow again to show the Timeline panel.

### Separating Panels

You can remove panels from their docked position to any other part of the workspace. Click and hold down your mouse button on the left-hand side of the panel title bar. The mouse pointer will change to a double-headed arrow and you will be able to drag the panel to any location on the screen.

You can minimize the panel by clicking the left arrow on the panel title bar. After you have done this, you will only be able to see the title bar.

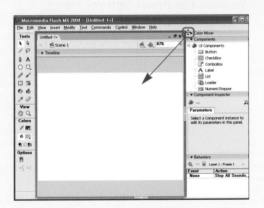

You can continue to drag panels away from their docked locations. Panels that are not docked are called floating panels.

### Merging Floating Panels

Floating panels can be joined together by dragging the left-hand side of the panel title bar. Move the panel to another panel and you will see a thick black line indicating that the panels are about to be joined. When you release your mouse button, both panels will be merged.

Merged Panel

### Minimizing Merged Panels

Merged panels can be minimized by clicking the arrow button to the left of the panel title.

Minimized Panel

# Creating Your Own Personal Workspace

We've covered some of the basic skills you'll need for Flash, and by now you should be comfortable working within the standard Flash environment. You can customize the workspace so that it suits your needs better by creating and saving your own panel set. You could even create multiple panel layouts and switch between them.

❶ Before you can save a panel set, you will need to arrange your panels on the screen. You might want to open some extra panels and close others. Some panels may be floating and others may be docked.

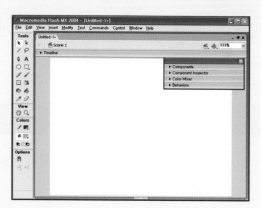

❷ You can save the panel layout by choosing [Windows] - [Save Panel Layout].

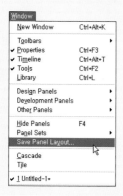

❸ To save the panel layout, you must name your panel set and click [OK].

❹ To test the new panel set, switch to another view such as the Default Layout. You can do this by choosing [Windows] - [Panel Sets] - [Default Layout]. The workspace should change accordingly.

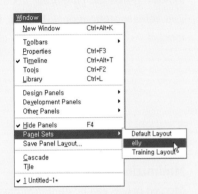

❺ Open your customized panel layout by going to [Windows] - [Panel Sets] and selecting the name of your panel set.

❻ The workspace should change to show your custom panel set.

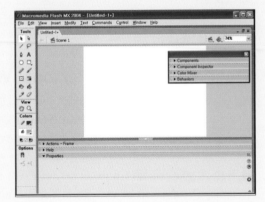

## Opening and Saving Flash Files

Before you start creating your own Flash movies, you'll need to learn how to work with files, including opening and saving them. Saving Flash files is an important skill and one that you should practice often so that you don't accidentally lose your work!

## Opening a Flash Movie

### Using the Start Page

The start page appears each time you open Flash and whenever you have no files open. It lists the files that you have recently worked on, making it much quicker to locate them. To open a file, click its title. If you can't see your filename in the list, you can browse for it by clicking [Open].

## Using the Menu

Another way to open files is to use [File] - [Open] from the menu bar at the top of the screen to select the file. You may have to use the drop-down menu at the top to locate the folder that contains your work.

For practice, open [Sample] - [Chapter01] - [01-001.fla] from the supplementary CD-ROM.

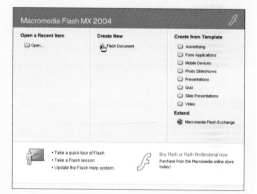

# Creating a New Movie

## Using the Start Page

To create a new blank movie, go to the Create New section and click the [Flash Document] option.

## Using the Menu

You can also select [File] - [New] in the menu bar to create a new movie.

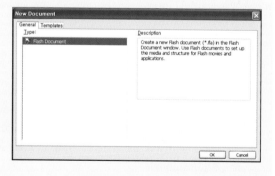

If you have several files open at the same time, the name of each file will display as a tab. You can use these tabs to switch between files.

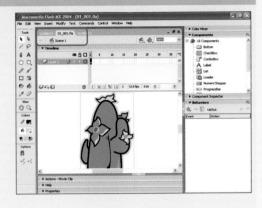

## Saving a Movie

It is important to get into the habit of saving your work regularly. This can help you avoid accidentally losing movies that you've worked hard on. It's also important to give some thought to how you name and organize your files. Using a good naming strategy and filing system can help you to find your movies later on.

❶ To save a file, choose [File] - [Save] from the menu bar.

❷ The first time you save a movie, you will be asked for the filename and location in the Save As dialog box. Choose Desktop from the drop-down menu at the top of the window. Click the [Create New Folder] icon and name it **flashmovie**.

❸ Double-click on the flashmovie folder, give your movie a filename, and click [Save]. When you return to your movie, the name will appear on the title bar at the top of the page. The next time you save this file, you won't be asked for the name and location again.

## Publishing a Movie

Before you can share your Flash movies with other people, you will need to publish your work. This creates files that can be played with Flash Player.

❶ To publish a movie, choose [File] - [Publish].

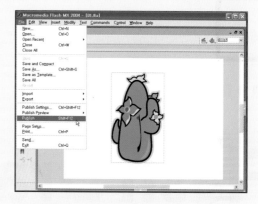

❷ You can view your published files by viewing the folder where the Flash movie is saved. Minimize Flash and open the flashmovie folder on the desktop. You will see that it contains three files, each with a different file extension. The FLA file is the Flash movie. This is the file that you'll work with in Flash. The HTML and SWF files are for use with Flash Player.

❸ By double–clicking the SWF file, you will be able to see the movie in the Flash player.

tip >>

Flash Player 7 is installed along with the Flash program. You can also view the movie on a Web page by double-clicking the HTML file.

Chapter 2

# Flash Drawing Techniques

Before you can start creating animations in Flash, you will need to learn how to draw the characters that you are going to animate. Flash comes with a set of customizable tools that you can use to draw the shapes that make up your animations. The key to drawing in Flash is learning how to use each of the tools in the toolbox properly. Most of the work that you'll do in Flash will require you to use drawing tools and to develop skills in editing shapes.

# Introduction

In this chapter, you will learn to use almost all of the tools in the toolbox, and you'll explore the options that are available for each tool. Towards the end of this section, you will learn about the Arrange, Align, and Trace Bitmap menu commands, which will give you more flexibility when drawing in Flash.

## Basic Drawing Tools

The basic drawing tools within Flash include the Line, Pencil, Oval, and Rectangle tools. When you draw with the Rectangle and Oval tools, you can create a line either around the outside of the shape, around the fill inside the shape, or around both at the same time. The Pencil and Line tools only create lines.

### The Line Tool ( )

The Line tool is used to draw straight lines and can be accessed by clicking the tool or by pressing the [n] key on the keyboard. After selecting this tool, the Property Inspector can be used to set the line color, thickness, and line type.

tip >>

**Drawing Horizontal, Vertical, and Diagonal Lines**

Hold down the [Shift] key with the Line tool to draw vertical, horizontal, and 45-degree lines.

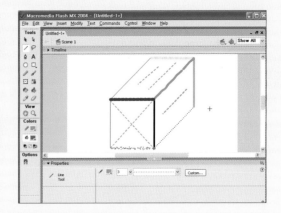

### The Pencil Tool ( )

The Pencil tool is used to draw free-form lines. Access this tool with the [y] key. You can set the line thickness, color, and type in the Property Inspector.

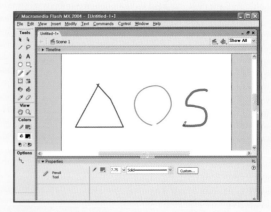

The options section of the toolbox contains settings that can be used to make lines smoother. There are three options—Straighten, Smooth, and Ink.

**Ⓐ Straighten**

Straighten converts the line into straight segments.

**Ⓑ Smooth**

Smooth makes the lines as smooth as possible, using gentle curves.

**Ⓒ Ink**

Ink makes the least changes to create natural-looking lines.


# The Oval Tool (⊙) and the Rectangle Tool (▢)

The Oval tool is used to draw ovals and circles while the Rectangle tool draws squares and rectangles. The Rectangle tool button also includes the PolyStar tool, which creates polygons and stars. The Property Inspector allows you to set the border line color, thickness, and type as well as the fill color for these tools.


## Using the Oval Tool (⊙)

The Oval tool can be accessed with the letter [o] on the keyboard. Set the properties for the tool using the Property Inspector and then click and drag on the stage to create an oval shape. If you hold down the [Shift] key at the same time, you will create a circle.

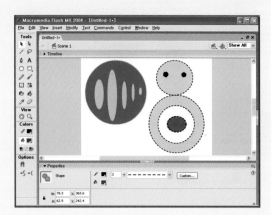


## Using the Rectangle Tool (▢)

The Rectangle tool works in a similar way to the Oval tool, and can be brought up with the letter [r] on the keyboard. After setting the properties for the tool, click and drag on the stage to create a rectangle. If you hold down the [Shift] key at the same time, you will create a square.

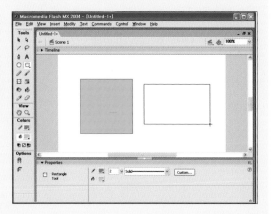

The Rectangle tool can also be used to draw rectangles and squares with rounded corners. Go to the Rectangle tool options in the toolbox and select [Round Rectangle Radius] to open the Rectangle Settings dialog box. Set the desired corner radius to add rounded corners.

### The Rectangle Settings Dialog Box

The corner radius values must be between 0 and 999. The larger the value, the more rounded the corners will be. If you make this value large enough, you can even draw a circle.

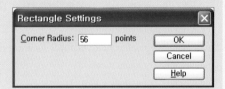

The Rectangle tool also includes the PolyStar tool (). If you click and hold the Rectangle tool, a menu will appear that allows you to choose between the Rectangle tool and the PolyStar tool.

You can change the PolyStar tool properties by going to the Property Inspector. In addition to the standard line and fill properties, the [Options] button in the Property Inspector brings up the Tool Settings dialog box with additional tool options.

The Tool Settings dialog box allows you to select the style of the tool, either polygon or star. You can enter the number of sides as well as the star point size.

Combining these options allows you to draw a range of different polygon and star shapes.

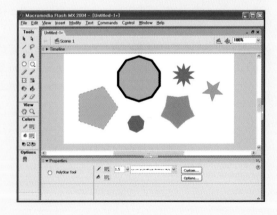

# Free-Form Drawing Tools

## The Brush Tool (✏️)

The Brush tool is used to apply color to objects. The brush size, shape, and color can be adjusted. There are different options that specify how color is to be applied. The Brush tool is activated by pressing the [b] key on the keyboard.

Right Graphic: Colored Using the Brush Tool

### Brush Tool Options

The Brush tool options appear in the options section of the toolbox.

**Brush Mode**

The Brush mode determines how paint will be applied to an object.

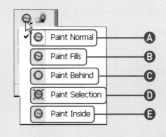

Ⓐ **Paint Normal**

Paints everything.

Ⓑ **Paint Fills**

Paints over fills or empty spaces. Does not paint over lines.

Ⓒ **Paint Behind**

Paints empty spaces. Ignores objects.

Ⓓ **Paint Selection**

Paints selected lines and fills. Does not paint in empty spaces.

Ⓔ **Paint Inside**

Paints only inside the area where painting with the Brush tool started.

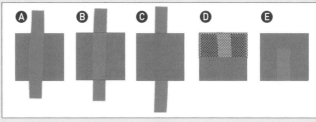

**Lock Fill (🔒)**

Lock Fill is used to treat separate objects as if they were connected when they are filled. For example, this will allow you to apply a single gradient to more than one object.

**Brush Size (●⌄)**

Sets the brush size.

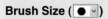

**Brush Shape (●⌄)**

Sets the brush shape.

# The Eraser Tool (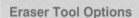)

The Eraser tool is used to erase lines and surfaces. It comes with five different modes and can be activated by pressing [e] on the keyboard.

## Eraser Tool Options

The Eraser tool options are used to set which part of the objects on stage will be erased.

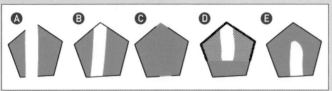

Examples of Each Eraser Mode

### Erase Mode ()

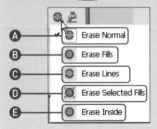

**Ⓐ Erase Normal**
Erases everything.

**Ⓑ Erase Fills**
Erases fills but ignores lines.

**Ⓒ Erase Lines**
Erases lines but ignores fills.

**Ⓓ Erase Selected Fills**
Erases fills inside the current selection.

**Ⓔ Erase Inside**
Erases only inside the area where erasing first started.

### Faucet (📛)

Click to erase complicated lines and fills.

### Erase Shape ( ● ∨ )

Sets the shape and size of the Eraser tool.

# The Text Tool (A)

The Text tool is used to add text to Flash files and can be loaded by pressing [t] on the keyboard. Click on the stage to add text. There are three types of text that can be added to your movies—static, dynamic, and input. Dynamic and input text types are normally used when programming Flash. Use the Property Inspector to adjust the font, font size, color, alignment, and spacing for your text.

## The Text Tool Property Inspector

**Ⓐ** Set text font

**Ⓑ** Set text size

**Ⓒ** Set text color

**Ⓓ** Bold text

**Ⓔ** Italic text

**Ⓕ** Set text direction

**Ⓖ** Set text alignment

**Ⓗ** Edit format option

**Ⓘ** Alias text

**Ⓙ** Auto Kern

**Ⓚ** Remove excess spacing from between letters

**Ⓛ** Set text spacing

If you want to edit an object drawn with the Line, Pencil, Oval, or Rectangle tools, you will have to select it first with either the Arrow or Lasso tools.

## Selecting Objects Using the Selection Tool ( )

### Making a Selection

#### Selecting Lines

Press the letter [v] on the keyboard to bring up the Selection tool. For an object made up of multiple lines, clicking the tool once on the object will select the clicked line. If you want to select all the lines in the object, double-click the object and all lines that connect to the clicked line will be selected at the same time.

Selecting One Line

Selecting All Lines

tip >>

If there is a break in the line, you can still double-click to make a selection.

#### Selecting Lines and Fills

Objects created with the Oval or Rectangle tools may be made up of both a line and a fill. You can either click the fill to select just that area, or double-click the fill to select both the lines and the fill.

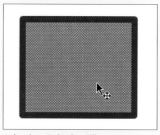

Selecting Only the Fill

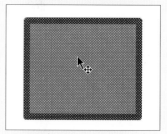

Selecting Both Lines and Fill

#### Making a Selection by Dragging

You can also drag the Selection tool to create a selection. Click and hold the mouse outside the object and drag it around the object. You will notice a selection outline. When you release the mouse, the area inside the outline will be selected. You can use this technique to select a whole object or even part of an object.

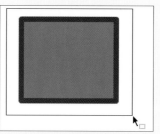

Dragging the Mouse

Selecting the Object by Dragging the Mouse

## Making Multiple Selections and Undoing Selections

You can add to your original selection by holding down the [Shift] key when you make the next selection. The [Shift] key can also be used to reduce the size of your selection. [Shift]-click an area that has already been selected to deselect it.

## Using the Selection Tool to Change Object Shape

In addition to making selections, the Selection tool can change the shape of an object. You can click and drag the lines and corners to change an object's shape.

### Changing Object Shape at Corners

Point to the corner of an object and drag to change the shape as shown here. The cursor will change to ⌐.

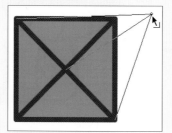 

### Changing Object Shape Using Lines

When you place the cursor over a line, the mouse cursor will change to ⌐. This can be used to bend or add curves to objects.

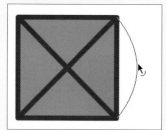 

## Using the Selection Tool to Copy Objects

The Selection tool can also create copies of an object. Select the object that is to be copied, hold down the [Ctrl] or [Alt] key, and drag the object to a new location. Your mouse pointer will display a + sign. As you move the object to another part of the stage, a copy of the original object will be created.

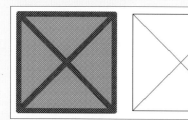 

Using the [Alt] Key to Copy

The Duplicated Object

## Selecting Objects Using the Lasso Tool ()

The Lasso tool can be used to make irregular selections. Type [l] on the keyboard to bring up the tool. You can then draw your selection on the stage. Do not release the mouse as you draw, and don't forget to close the selection!

Making a Selection Using the Lasso Tool

An Area Selected Using the Lasso Tool

## Editing Bitmaps

The Lasso tool is especially useful for editing bitmap images because you can make detailed selections, as shown in the example below.

1 Select [File] - [Import] - [Import to Stage] to load a bitmap image into your movie. Select [Modify] - [Break Apart] from the menu or use the shortcut keys [Ctrl]-[B]. Use the Lasso tool to select the desired area within the image.

2 Remove the background and display only the selected image on the screen.

### Lasso Tool Options

The Lasso tool can be used in other ways, depending on the options selected in the toolbox.

### Magic Wand

The Magic Wand selects areas of color that are similar to, and touching, the clicked area. This tool can be used in bitmap images to make a selection based on the colors in the image. You may want to hold down the [Shift] key to add to your original selection.

### Magic Wand Settings

You can determine how closely the Magic Wand matches the clicked color by changing the Magic Wand settings. The higher the Threshold value, the more image will be selected. Smoothing determines how smooth the selection edges will be.

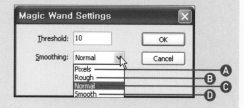

**A Pixels**: The selection uses the rectangular edges of pixels.

**B Rough**: An angular selection is created, with an edge harder than in the Pixels setting.

**C Normal**: The selection is softer than the Pixels setting but rougher than the Smooth setting.

**D Smooth**: The selection edges are rounded.

### Polygon Mode

In Polygon mode, the Lasso tool creates polygonal or straight-line selections. Click the tool to mark the corners of the polygon. Double-click the last point to make the selection.

## Advanced Drawing and Editing Tools

## The Pen Tool ( ) and the Subselection Tool ( )

The Pen and Subselection tools allow the creation of detailed objects. These tools are often used together to create curves, and they both take practice to master.

### Using the Pen Tool to Draw ( )

The Pen tool is used to create a series of points that are joined by either straight or curved lines. These are known as bezier curves. It may take a little practice to get the hang of the Pen tool.

## Drawing Straight Lines

Select the Pen tool by pressing the [p] key on the keyboard. Configure the line color and thickness in the Property Inspector and click the workspace to create the starting point for your line. Click the second point and a line will be created to connect the two points.

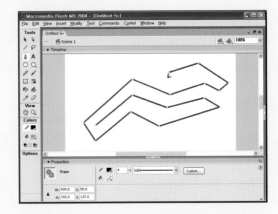

## Drawing Bezier Curves

Using the Pen tool to draw curves is a little more complicated than drawing straight lines. Load the Pen tool, then click (and hold) the mouse button over the workspace to create a starting point. Drag the mouse over the workspace with the mouse button pressed to determine the direction and severity of your curve. Release the mouse button, then click-and-drag again to create a second point in your outline. The curve properies of this second point will be blended with those of the first to create a curved line between the two points. Continue to drag line segments to add to the drawing.

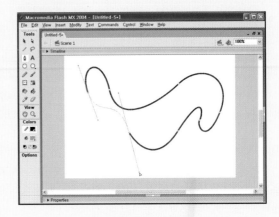

You will notice that handles appear as you create the curves. If you hold down the [Shift] key as you drag the Pen tool, you will create horizontal, vertical, and 45-degree handles.

### The Elements of a Bezier Curve

Curves drawn with the Pen tool will have anchor points and tangent handles.

**Anchor Points**

Anchor points are created wherever the Pen tool is clicked. They represent the start and finish of a section of the curve.

**Tangent Handles**

Tangent handles are the directional lines that appear at anchor points. You can drag the handles to adjust the curve.

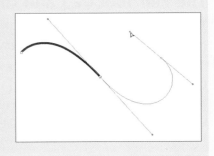

### Using the Subselection Tool to Edit ( )

Objects drawn using the Line, Pencil, Oval, Rectangle, and Pen tools have anchor points that can be selected with the Subselection tool. Press [a] to bring up this tool. Try out the example below:

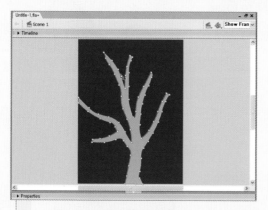

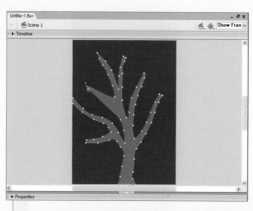

1 When you click with the Subselection tool, the anchor points for the object will appear.

2 You can drag a point with the mouse to move it to a new location, or you can use the [Left], [Right], [Up], and [Down] arrow keys on the keyboard to nudge a selected point.

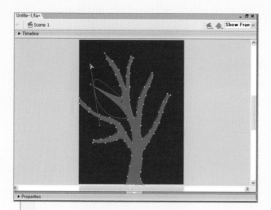

3 You can also drag the endpoints of the handles to change the shape of the curve. Both handles will move at the same time. If you want to adjust one of the handles, hold down the [Alt] key while dragging.

# The Free Transform Tool ( )

The Free Transform tool is used to change the skew, scale, rotation, and distortion of objects on the stage. Press the letter [q] on the keyboard to use the tool. There are four options for using the tool within the Options section of the toolbox—rotate and skew ( ), scale ( ), distort ( ), and envelope ( ).

To use the Free Transform tool, select the object on the stage and click the tool's button. Choose the type of transformation you want to apply from the Options section. You can also use the tool to click on the object that you want to transform. Once the Free Transform tool is applied to an object, it will show black handles that can be used for transformations.

### Rotating an Object

You can use the standard Free Transform tool ($\boxminus$) to rotate an object. Click outside one of the corners of the object, and the mouse cursor will change into a rotate cursor ($\circlearrowright$). Drag the mouse to rotate the object.

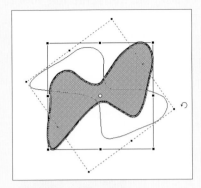

### Skew Transform ($\overline{\partial}$)

To use the skew transform, drag the center handle of a side to create a skewed effect.

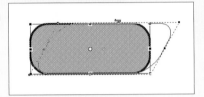

### Scale Transform ($\boxed{\nearrow}$)

The scale transformation is applied by selecting one of the black squares and dragging it to change the size of the object. If you drag a corner and hold down the [Shift] key, the object will retain its proportions.

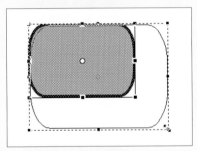

### Distort Transform ($\boxed{\nearrow}$)

The distort transformation allows you to drag each of the black squares independently of each other to distort the overall shape of the object. Holding down the [Shift] key allows you to transform the object symmetrically.

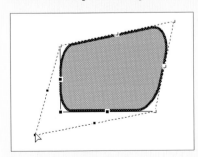
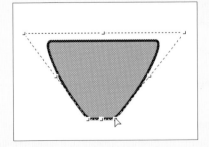

## Envelope Transform ( 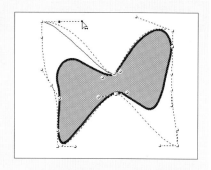 )

The envelope transformation uses both circular and rectangular handles to transform the shape. Circular handles contain tangent handles to create curves. Rectangular handles move the points to act like a distortion transformation.

---

**tip >>**

### Limits of Free-Transform Options

Skew Transform ( ) and Scale Transform ( ) can be applied to all objects, but Distort Transform ( ) and Envelope Transform ( ) only work on shapes drawn with the Oval, Rectangle, Pencil, and Pen tools. Distort Transform and Envelope Transform can't be applied to grouped shapes or symbols.

### The Transform Menu

Another way to transform a selected object on the stage is to use the [Modify] - [Transform] menu.

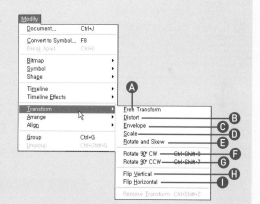

**A Free Transform**

Activates the Free Transform tool.

**B Distort**

Activates the Free Transform tool with the Distort option selected in the toolbox.

**C Envelope**

Activates the Free Transform tool with the Envelope option selected in the toolbox.

**D Scale**

Activates the Free Transform tool with the Scale option selected in the toolbox.

**E Rotate and Skew**

Activates the Free Transform tool with the Rotate and Skew option selected in the toolbox.

**F Rotate 90° CW**

Rotates the selected object clockwise by 90 degrees.

**G Rotate 90° CCW**

Rotates the selected object counterclockwise by 90 degrees.

**H Flip Vertical**

Flips the selected object vertically (i.e., the top and bottom positions are reversed).

**I Flip Horizontal**

Flips the selected object horizontally (i.e., the left and right positions are reversed).

# The Paint Bucket Tool (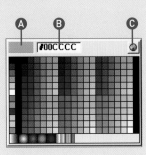)

The Paint Bucket tool fills an object with color. The [k] key on the keyboard activates this tool.

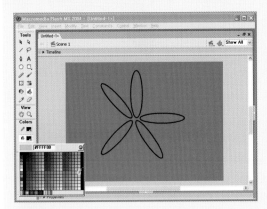

## Color Palette

Ⓐ **Color Preview**: Displays the selected color.

Ⓑ **Hexadecimal Text Box**: Displays the color value in the form of a hexadecimal number.

Ⓒ **System Color Picker**: Allows users to create custom colors.

# Mixing and Saving Your Own Color

You can mix your own color instead of using the current swatches in the color palette.

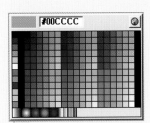
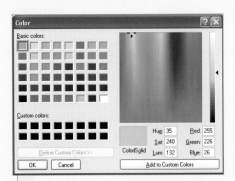

1 In the color palette, click on the [System Color Picker] button (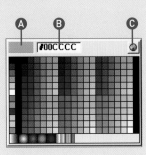).

2 The Color window will appear. Select the color from the color space or enter the color value in the RGB (red, green, blue) or HSL (hue, saturation, luminosity) fields. If you want to save a new color that you have mixed, select a swatch under Custom Colors and click the [Add to Custom Colors] button.

**tip >>**

**I Can't Color the Object!**

If the Paint Bucket tool can't fill your object, it's probably because you have gaps in the shape. The Paint Bucket tool works best with closed shapes. You can either fill in the gaps before using this tool or use the options section of the Paint Bucket tool to change the Close Gaps setting.

## Paint Bucket Tool Options

The options section of the toolbox provides some different ways for the Paint Bucket tool to deal with gaps in the selected object.

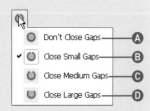

Ⓐ **Don't Close Gaps**

Colors only completely closed shapes.

Ⓑ **Close Small Gaps**

Colors shapes with very tiny gaps.

Ⓒ **Close Medium Gaps**

Colors shapes with medium-sized gaps.

Ⓓ **Close Large Gaps**

Colors shapes with large gaps. There is a limit to how large a gap Flash can deal with, so it is better to make the gaps as small as possible.

# The Ink Bottle Tool (🖋)

The Ink Bottle tool is used to specify line color, thickness, and shape. The tool can also be used to add a border to a borderless object. It is activated with the [s] key on the keyboard.

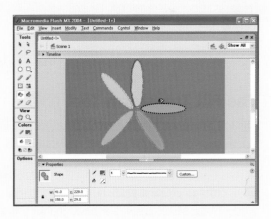

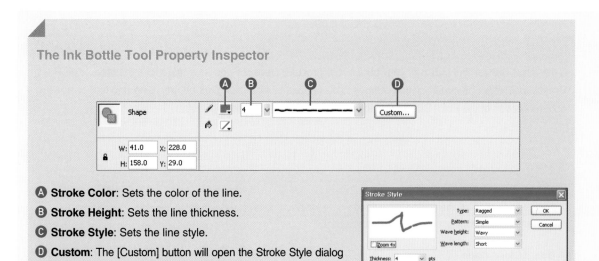

**The Ink Bottle Tool Property Inspector**

Ⓐ **Stroke Color**: Sets the color of the line.

Ⓑ **Stroke Height**: Sets the line thickness.

Ⓒ **Stroke Style**: Sets the line style.

Ⓓ **Custom**: The [Custom] button will open the Stroke Style dialog box to allow you to create user-defined styles.

## The Eyedropper Tool (🖉)

The Eyedropper tool is used to sample color from an object on the stage so you can apply it to another object. The tool can also sample from a bitmap image.

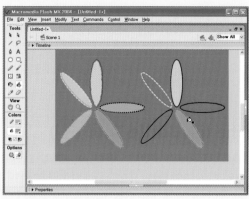

Sample the line and fill color of the object on the left, and apply it to the object on the right.

## The Fill Transform Tool (🗔)

The Fill Transform tool is used on gradients. When an object has been filled with a gradient, the tool allows you to scale or rotate the gradient. The tool doesn't change the shape of the object and can be activated by pressing [f] on the keyboard.

❶ In order to create a gradient, select a fill style from the Color Mixer panel. For now, choose a linear or radial gradient.

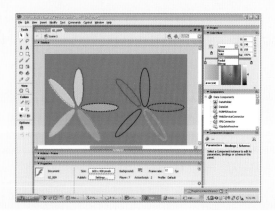

❷ Select each of the pointers below the Gradient Definition bar and choose a color in the color space.

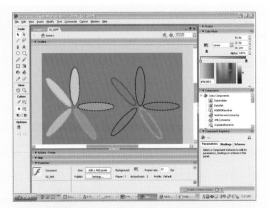

❸ Drag the Brightness control to adjust the brightness.

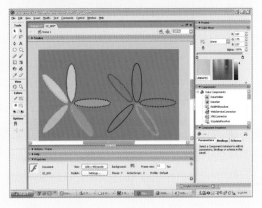

❹ You can drag the pointers to a new location or add more pointers by clicking between the existing pointers. Pointers can be removed by dragging them out of the Color Mixer panel.

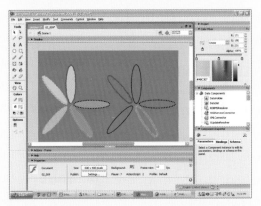

# Applying and Transforming Gradients

In this section, let's use the following example to explore the different ways that gradients can be applied and transformed.

## Radial Gradients

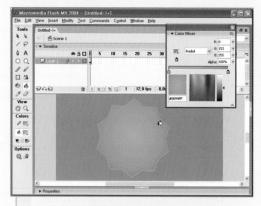

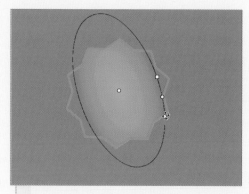

1 Apply a radial gradient by selecting the Paint Bucket tool and changing the fill style to radial. Select the colors for the gradient and add the gradient by clicking the Paint Bucket tool inside the shape.

2 Click the gradient with the Fill Transform tool () to activate three Fill Transform handles. The top handle is used to change the width of the fill. The middle handle increases and decreases the size of the fill, and the bottom handle rotates the gradient. You can move the fill by clicking and dragging on the center point.

## Linear Gradients

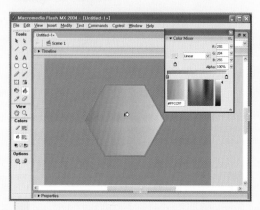

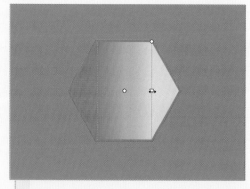

1 A linear gradient can also by applied using the Paint Bucket tool. Change the fill style setting to linear and select the colors for the gradient. Add the gradient by clicking the Paint Bucket tool inside the shape.

2 Click the gradient with the Fill Transform tool () to activate two Fill Transform handles. The top handle is used to rotate the fill. The other handle increases and decreases the width. You can drag the center point to move the fill to a new location.

## Arranging and Aligning Objects on the Stage

Other than the tools, you will need to use two other menu commands frequently when drawing in Flash. These two commands are the Arrange and Align commands, which are found on the [Modify] menu.

## Arranging Objects

You can arrange symbols on the stage using the [Modify] - [Arrange] menu. The first four arrange options allow you to change the stacking order of objects that are located in the same place on the stage. Using these options is a little like shuffling the order of a stack of cards to reveal some cards and hide others.

### The Arrange Menu

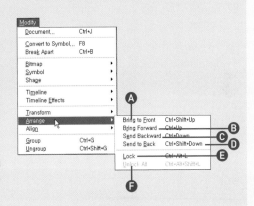

**Ⓐ Bring to Front**
Brings the selected object to the front of the stage, on top of any other objects in the same location.

**Ⓑ Bring Forward**
Brings the selected object one "layer" forward. You can repeat this option to move the selected object to the top of all the objects.

**Ⓒ Send Backward**
Moves the selected object one "layer" backward. You can repeat this option to move the selected object to the bottom of all the objects.

**Ⓓ Send to Back**
Moves the selected object to the bottom of all the other objects in the same location.

**Ⓔ Lock**
Locks the selected object so that it cannot be selected.

**Ⓕ Unlock All**
Unlocks all locked objects.

## Aligning Objects

The Align panel allows you to arrange a group of objects on the stage. You can bring up the panel by selecting [Window] - [Design Panels] - [Align] or with the shortcut keys [Ctrl]-[K]. The same options are also available within the [Modify] - [Align] menu.

### The Align Panel

**Ⓐ Align buttons**: The first three buttons deal with left-to-right alignment.
*Left align* - Aligns selected objects with the object furthest to the left.
*Horizontal center alignment* - Aligns selected objects across the center.
*Right align* - Aligns selected objects with the object furthest to the right.

The last three align buttons deal with top-to-bottom alignment.

*Top align* - Aligns selected objects with the object closest to the top of the stage.

*Vertical center alignment* - Aligns selected objects across the middle.

*Bottom align* - Aligns selected objects with the object closest to the bottom of the stage.

**B** **Distribute buttons**: The Distribute buttons control the way that the space between selected objects is distributed. From left to right, the buttons are Top distribution, Horizontal center distribution, Bottom distribution, Left distribution, Vertical center distribution, and Right distribution.

**C** **Match size**: The Match Size buttons allow you to change the size of the selected objects to the same height (Vertical match), width (Horizontal match), or both (Vertical and Horizontal match).

**D** **Space**: The two Space buttons allow you to space out selected objects evenly, either vertically or horizontally.

**E** **To stage**: This button is used with the Distribute buttons. When checked, the selected objects are distributed according to the height or width of the stage. Otherwise, distribution is calculated by the farthest positions of the selected objects.

# Using the Trace Bitmap Command

The Trace Bitmap command lets you work with bitmap images by converting an imported bitmap into a vector image. You can bring up the Trace Bitmap dialog box by selecting [Modify] - [Bitmap] - [Trace Bitmap]. Tracing an image will almost always reduce the quality of the original bitmap.

## The Trace Bitmap Dialog Box

**A** **Color threshold**: This setting determines which color values are rounded off to the same color. The higher the number, the fewer the number of different colors in the traced vector image

**B** **Minimum area**: The minimum area indicates how many surrounding pixels will be averaged to determine a pixel's color. The higher the number, the fewer unique colors there will be in the vector image.

**C** **Curve fit**: The closer the option in the drop-down is to the bottom, the less detail and the smoother the lines will be in the vector image. Choosing a more detailed option will increase the file size.

**D** **Corner threshold**: The closer the option is to the bottom, the fewer the corners in the image and the smaller the file size.

You will probably have to experiment with different settings before you are satisfied with the final result. To remove the tracing, use the [Ctrl]-[Z] shortcut and reapply the Trace Bitmap with new settings.

# Text Design

Flash can be used to create many different types of text designs. In this section, you'll use Flash to create effects such as a gradient fill and three-dimensional text.

**Start File**
　\Sample\Chapter02\02_001.fla

**Final File**
　\Sample\Chapter02\02_001_end.fla

1　Select [File] - [Open] and open the start file. Use the Selection tool to select the first UNIVERSE SPACE on the stage. You will notice that the text has been broken apart into letter shapes.

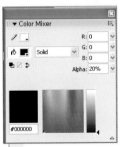

2　Use the [Shift]-[F9] shortcut keys to open the Color Mixer panel. Set the fill color to #000000 and the alpha value to 20%.

**3** Press [Ctrl]-[G] to group the letters. Use the Free Transform tool (⊞) to make the text taller as shown below.

**4** In the Color Mixer panel, set the fill style to Linear. Click below the gradient line to add two more color points. There should be four color points in the gradient. Set the color values to #9EBCEB, #42ECEC, #9451CC, and #CCE36A from left to right.

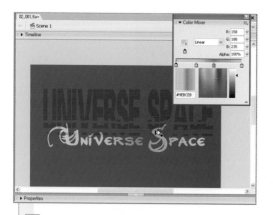

**5** Select the UNIVERSE SPACE text at the bottom of the stage and use the Paint Bucket tool (🪣) to fill the text with the gradient.

**6** Using the Selection tool, hold down the [Alt] key and drag the gradient text to the bottom of the stage. This will create a copy.

**7** Change the fill style of the copied text to Solid and set the fill color to #000000. Set the alpha value to 100%.

**8** Use [Ctrl]-[C] to copy the black text. Press [Ctrl]-[Shift]-[V] to paste the copy in place. Press the left and up arrow keys once each to nudge the text to a new location.

**9** Copy and paste the text in place again. Nudge the text as before. Repeat step 8 four more times. Select all copies and use [Ctrl]-[G] to group the objects together.

**10** Select the colored UNIVERSE SPACE text and group the shapes with the [Ctrl]-[G] shortcut. Move the text as shown below to create a three dimensional effect.

**11** Select the Text tool ([A]). In the Property Inspector, set the font to Arial, the font size to 62 pt, and the font color to #FFFFFF. Type the word **Heaven** on the stage.

**12** Use the Selection tool to select the Heaven text and press [Ctrl]-[B] twice to break apart the text and create letter shapes. Hold down the [Alt] key and drag the Heaven text to the bottom of the stage to create a copy.

**13** Change the fill color of the top Heaven text to #FF0000. Click the stage to deselect the text, then select the Ink Bottle tool ([🖊]). Set the stroke color to #FFFFFF and use the tool to add a border to the red Heaven text. Click on the stage to deselect the text.

**14** Select the Heaven text copy at the bottom of the stage. Choose [Modify] - [Shape] - [Soften Fill Edges].

65

15 Set the distance to 14, the number of steps to 8, the direction to Expand, and click [OK].

16 Use the [Ctrl]-[G] shortcut to group the softened text.

17 Select the top Heaven text, then hold down the [Alt] key to drag to make a copy. Use the Free Transform tool (⊞) to increase the size of the text. Position all of the Heaven text as shown above.

18 Press [Ctrl]-[Enter] to preview the movie.

## Let's Go Pro!

If you open a Flash movie containing fonts that you do not have on your computer, font mapping will substitute a font for the missing font.

**Start File**

\Sample\Chapter02\02_002.fla

# A New Feature - Font Mapping

**01** When you open the start file on your computer, you should see the Missing Font Warning dialog box. Click the [Choose Substitute] button.

**02** In the Font Mapping dialog box, select the missing font Floralies and click the [Substitute Font] drop-down menu to select a replacement. Click [OK].

**03** The start file will be opened using the substitute font you selected. In this case, we chose the Godzilla font.

**04** If you are curious about the Floralies font, this is what it would look like without the font substitution.

tip >>

### [Use Default] Button

When the [Use Default] button is pressed in the Missing Font Warning dialog box, the default system font will be used as the substitute.

# 2

# Creating Logos with Text

Flash MX 2004 makes creating special effects with text much easier than in previous versions. In this section, we'll use the Text tool with the Transform tool to create a text logo.

3 Using the Property Inspector, change the font to Arial, the size to 52 pt, and the text (fill) color to White.

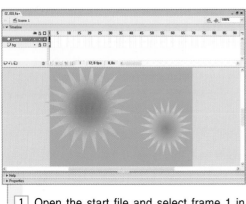

1 Open the start file and select frame 1 in Layer 1.

2 Select the Text tool ( A ) and click in the middle of the stage. Enter, **Want to go for a spin?**

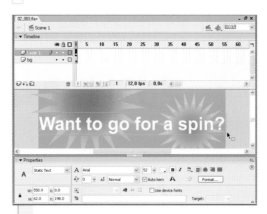

4 Use the Selection tool to select the text field. The text appears as a group.

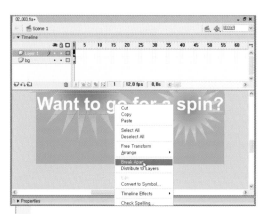

tip >>

**Shortcut Key**

The shortcut key for the Break Apart command is [Ctrl]-[B].

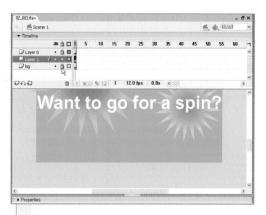

5 Right-click the text and select [Break Apart] from the shortcut menu.

6 The text is broken down into individual letters.

7 Right-click and apply Break Apart again to turn each letter into a shape.

8 Press the [Add Layer] icon (🖉) to add a new layer. Select frame 1 in Layer 1, hold down the [Alt] key, and drag frame 1 to the new layer.

9 Lock the bg layer and the new layer. Activate Layer 1 by clicking it.

tip >>

Moving frames while holding down the [Alt] key will make a copy of the frame in the new location.

tip >>

Click on the [Lock] icon for each layer to lock the corresponding layer.

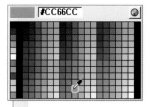

10 Select the Ink Bottle tool and set the stroke color to #CC66CC.

See Chapter 3 for more information on layers.

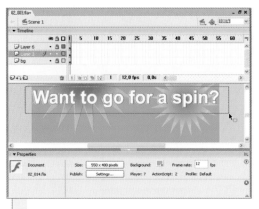

11 Click on the edge of each letter to add a border. You will have to click both the inside and outside edges for the letters **o**, **g,** and **a**.

12 Using the Selection tool, drag a selection around all of the text.

13 In the Property Inspector, set the stroke height to 6 pt.

14 Select the bg layer and click on the [Add Layer] icon to add a new layer.  Hold down the [Alt] key and copy the frame from the layer above into the new layer.  Lock the frame above.

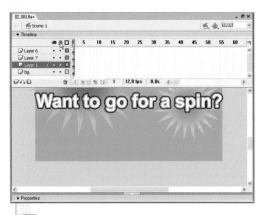

15 Select all of the text and change the stroke color to black and the stroke height to 10 pt in the Property Inspector.

16 Unlock all the locked layers except the bg layer by clicking the [Lock] icon (⬛) next to each locked layer.

17 Minimize the timeline and the Property Inspector to create more room for the stage. Click on [Show Frame] from the [Zoom] menu located above the timeline.

18 Choose the Selection tool ( ) from the toolbox and drag a selection over the text from the top-left corner of the text to the lower-right corner. This will select all of the text on all layers.

19 Choose the Free Transform tool ( ) and select the [Distort] option ( ) from the Options section in the toolbox. Use the tool to distort each corner of the text as shown here. Make sure the 'Want' side is bigger than the 'spin' side.

20 Select the [Envelope] option ( ) to transform the text even more. As shown, move the center point down and adjust the handles at each point to create a curved shape.

21 Press [Ctrl]-[Enter] to test the movie.

tip >>

### Undo

- **Using Shortcut Keys**
  If you've made a mistake and want to undo the last step, you can use the shortcut keys [Ctrl]-[Z]. Repeat this shortcut to undo more than one step.

- **Using Menus**
  You can also undo the last step using [Edit] - [Undo] from the menu bar.

- **Using the History Panel**
  The History panel contains a list of all the actions you've carried out in the current movie. You can click a step in the panel to return to that point.

Undoing a Step Using the History Panel

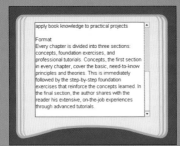

# Making a Scrolling Text Box

A popular use for components is to create a scrolling text box using the ScrollBar component. This component was provided with Flash MX, but is no longer included in Flash MX 2004. However, the start file includes the component within its library.

tip >>

## What is the Components Panel?

The Components panel contains special Flash movie clips called components. Flash MX 2004 includes components for creating user interfaces, such as checkboxes and push buttons. You can also add components from the Internet.

**01** Open the start file and select the Text tool (A). In the Property Inspector, enter these settings:

| [TEXT TYPE] | 'Dynamic Text' |
|---|---|
| Font | Arial |
| Size | 14pt |
| Font color | #000000 (black) |
| Line Type | Multiline |

**02** Click the [Show Border around Text] button to add a black border. Drag a text box on the stage as shown below.

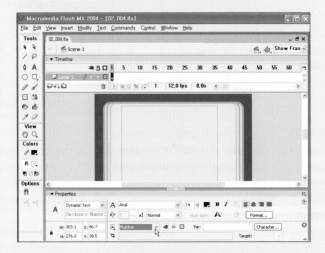

*03* Select the text box. Go to the Property Inspector and enter **scroll_text** for the instance name.

note >>

Instance names are given to dynamic and input text fields so that they can be manipulated with ActionScript. This feature was introduced in Flash MX.

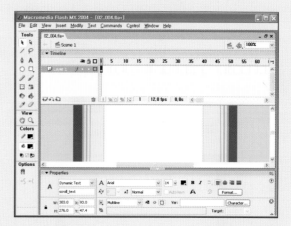

## Text Types

There are three different types of text fields that can be created in Flash: static, dynamic, and input.

**Ⓐ Static Text**
Static text is the most commonly used type of text field. It is selected when you want to type in the text that will be displayed on the stage.

**Ⓑ Dyamic Text**
A dynamic text field allows the content to be modified with ActionScript. It is often used by programmers.

**Ⓒ Input Text**
An input text field allows the user to enter their own text.

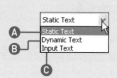

*04* Press [Ctrl]-[L] to open the library. Drag the ScrollBar movie onto the stage beside the text field. If you drop it onto the text box, it will automatically associate itself with that instance name in the Property Inspector.

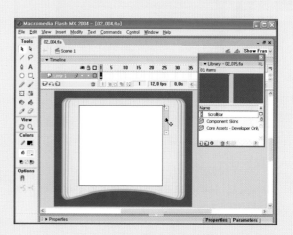

**05** Right-click the text field and select [Scrollable] from the shortcut menu. This will enable the scrollbar to work.

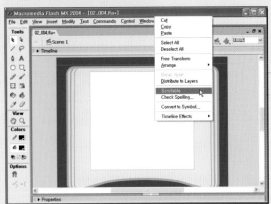

**06** Enter a long body of text.

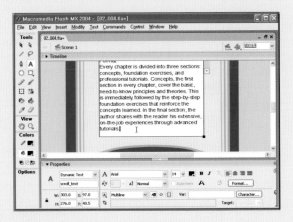

**07** Use the Selection tool to select the ScrollBar on the stage, press [Shift]-[Q] to activate the Free Transform tool (▦), then scale it so that it is the same height as the text box.

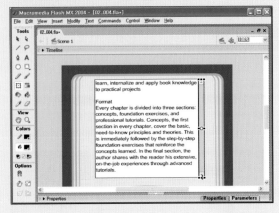

**08** Click on the ScrollBar and make sure that **scroll_text** is entered in the Target TextField of the Property Inspector.

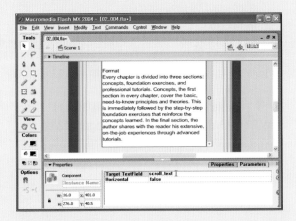

**09** Press [Ctrl]-[Enter] to test the movie. Check to see that the scrollbar in the text box works properly.

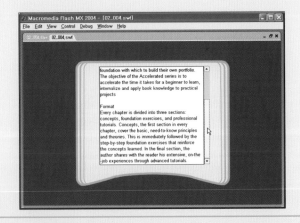

## Spell Checker

**①** Flash MX 2004 includes a spell checker. To use it, right-click the text box and select [Check Spelling...].

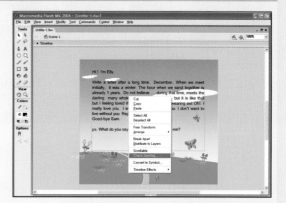

**②** The Check Spelling dialog box allows you to correct your spelling, ignore words, or add them to your personal dictionary. Each time Flash finds a word that it doesn't recognize, you can choose what action to take.

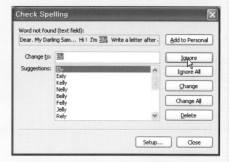

**③** After the spell check is complete, click [Close].

*Exercise*

# 3  Drawing a Rabbit

Drawing images in Flash requires a lot of practice. This section uses the example of drawing a rabbit to help you become more familiar with Flash's drawing tools. In addition to its drawing tools, Flash provides options that allow you to change the arrangement, position, and alignment of a symbol.

**Start File**
  ● \Sample\Chapter02\02_005.fla

**Final File**
  ● \Sample\Chapter02\02_005_end.fla

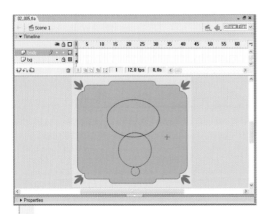

1  Open the start file and select frame 1 of the Body layer.

2  Select the Oval tool (○) and set the fill colors to no color. Draw a large oval at the top, a circle in the middle, and a small circle at the bottom as shown above.

3  Next, draw in an elongated oval in the empty space on the left. This shape will be used for the rabbit's ears. Draw a figure eight.

**note >>**

You can also access the Rectangle Settings dialog box by selecting the Rectangle tool and clicking the [Round Rectangle Radius] icon (⌐) in the options at the bottom of the toolbox.

4  Double-click the Rectangle tool. In the Rectangle Settings dialog box, set the corner radius to 20 points and click [OK].

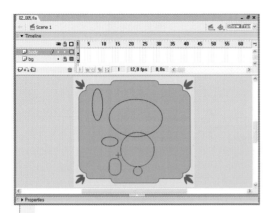

5   Use the Rectangle tool to draw one of the feet as shown above.

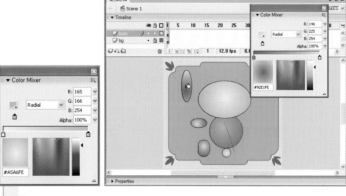

6   Press [Shift]-[F9] to open the Color Mixer panel, then set the fill style to radial and select the start and end colors for the gradient.

7   Click the Paint Bucket tool and color all the objects that have been drawn.

note >>

You could use any colors for the gradients. However, it looks best if you use similar color tones at the start and end points. When coloring the ears, the middle color should be darker than the outside color, whereas for the other objects, the middle color should be lighter than the outside color.

tip >>

Holding down the [Alt] key makes a copy of the selected object as it is dragged. Holding down the [Shift] key as well creates the copy at the same horizontal level as the original object.

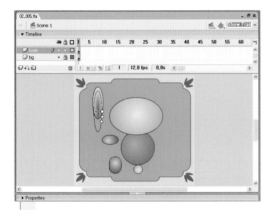

8   Use the Fill Transform tool to adjust the color gradients. Make sure that you adjust the scale so that the darker color is fully visible and is moved towards the bottom of the ear shape.

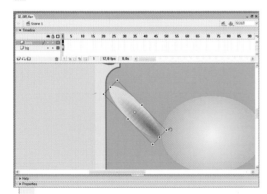

9   Rotate the ear shape about 45° using the Free Tranform tool. After making the adjustments, remove all borders by clicking them with the Selection tool and pressing the [Delete] key.

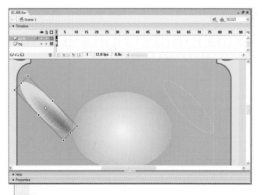

10   Select the oval that was created for the ear. Hold down the [Alt] key and drag it to the opposite side of the stage. This will create a copy of the ear.

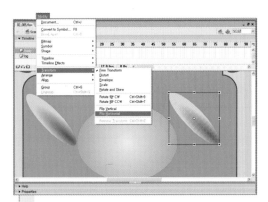

11 To create a mirror image of the first ear, select [Modify] - [Transform] - [Flip Horizontal] from the menu.

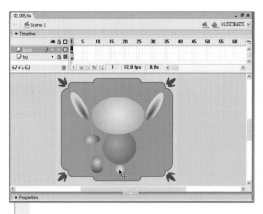

12 Select the three circles in the middle and press [Ctrl]-[G] to group them together. You can hold down the [Shift] key as you click each object with the Select tool to add it to the selection.

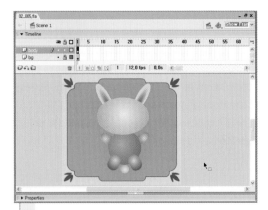

13 Place the two ears on either side of the head as shown above.

14 Place the foot on the body as shown above. See steps 10 and 11 to create the other foot.

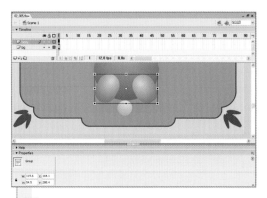

15 Select both feet and press [Ctrl]-[G] to group them together.

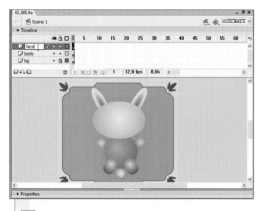

16 Add a layer to the timeline. Click frame 1 of the new layer, select the Oval tool, and set the fill color to #000000. Draw in both eyes.

note >>

The most recent group of objects will be placed above any existing groups. The feet group will be placed on top of the body group we made in step 11.

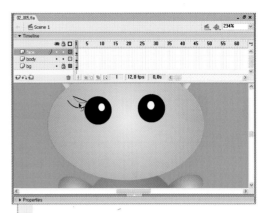

17 Change the fill color to #FFFFFF to draw the whites of the eyes.

18 Press [N] to activate the Line tool and then draw in the eyelashes as shown. Press [V] to activate the Selection tool and then drag the lines of the eyelashes so that they curve downwards. Repeat for the other eye.

19 Press [N] to activate the Line tool and set the stroke height to 2 pt. Draw in the whiskers as shown above.

20 Activate the Pen tool by pressing [P] and draw in the mouth as shown above.

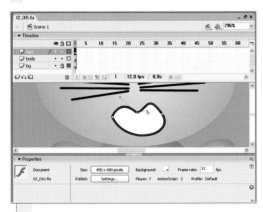

21 Choose the Subselection tool, hold down the [Alt] key, and drag the handles to adjust the top part of the mouth. Finish the mouth shape by adding a white fill and removing the lines.

22 Choose the white pupil in the left eye and select [Modify] - [Shape] - [Soften Fill Edges] from the menu.

23 In the Soften Fill Edges dialog box, set the distance to 6 px, the number of steps to 4, the direction to Expand, and click [OK].

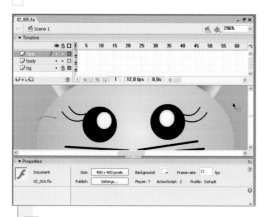

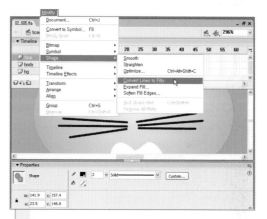

24 Repeat steps 22 and 23 for the other eye.

25 Select all six lines that were drawn for the whiskers and choose [Modify] - [Shape] - [Convert Lines to Fills]. The whiskers will change into filled shapes rather than lines.

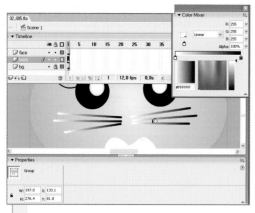

26 Make sure that the whiskers are still selected. In the Color Mixer panel, set the fill style to linear and make a black-to-white gradient. The whiskers should change as shown.

27 Use the Fill Transform tool on each side to make sure that the black part of the whiskers is nearest the middle of the face.

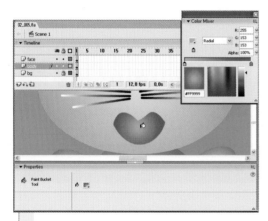

**28** Create a red gradient in the Color Mixer panel. Use the Paint Bucket tool to color the lips.

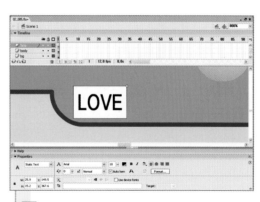

**29** Click the Text tool ( A ) and type in the word **LOVE** below the rabbit.

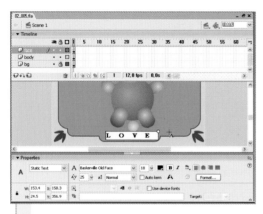

**30** In the Property Inspector, change the character spacing to 25 to space out the text.

**31** Press [Ctrl]-[Enter] to test the movie.

---

tip >>

## Making Small Text Easier to Read with Alias Text

The [Alias Text] icon ( A ) in the Property Inspector of the Text tool changes smooth text into pixel squares. Smooth text is more readable at large font sizes, but at small font sizes, pixel squares make small text more legible.

Excuse me, wha

Excuse me, wh:

Anti-Alias Text(top), Alias Text(bottom)

# Working with Bitmap Images

Although Flash is designed primarily for use with vector images, it can also be used with bitmap images such as JPEG and GIF files. You can convert a bitmap image into a vector image by using the Trace Bitmap command within Flash. You can also break a bitmap into blocks of color.

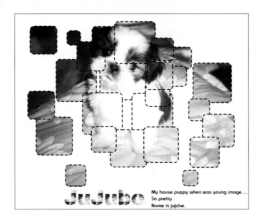

## Using a Bitmap to Fill Shapes

In this exercise, you will create a poster within Flash using a bitmap image to fill shapes and text.

**Final File**
\Sample\Chapter02\02_006_end.fla

**Import File**
\Sample\Chapter02\image\mypet.jpg

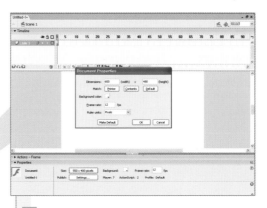

1 Select [File] - [New] from the menu or select [Create New] - [Flash Document] from the start page. In the Property Inspector, change the document size to 600 x 480 pixels..

2 Select [File] - [Import] - [Import to Stage] to add the bitmap image to the stage.

3 Select the file **mypet.jpg** and click [Open].

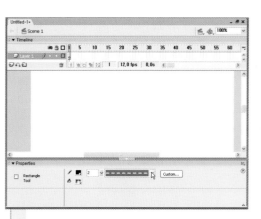

4 Select the imported image and press [Ctrl]-[B] to break apart the image. This converts the image into blocks of color that can be selected with the Eyedropper tool.

5 Use the Eyedropper tool to sample the image. This will allow you to use the bitmap as a fill for any shapes you add to the stage.

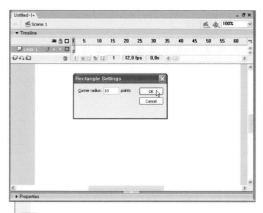

6 Delete the dog image and double-click the Rectangle tool to bring up the Rectangle Settings dialog box. Change the corner radius value to 10 and click [OK].

7 In the Property Inspector, set the stroke style to dotted line and the color to #000000.

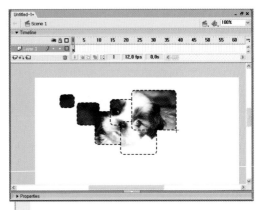

8　Draw several rectangles on the new layer stage as shown here. They should fill with the sampled bitmap image.

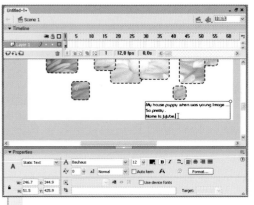

9　Select the Text tool and type in a message of your choice in the bottom-right corner.

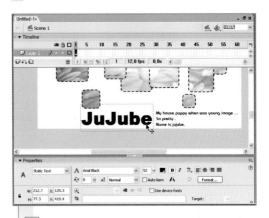

10　Type in **JuJube** as shown.　Set the font size to 52 pt and the font to Arial Black.

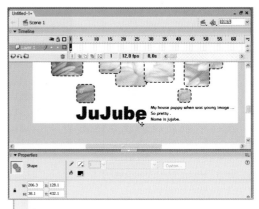

11　Select the text and press [Ctrl]-[B] twice to change the letters into shapes.

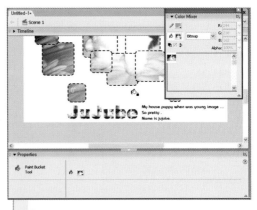

12　Select all of the text shapes in JuJube and set the fill style to Bitmap in the Color Mixer panel.

13　Press [Ctrl]-[Enter] to test the movie.

**About Import**

Import allows you to add external files into Flash including bitmap images, sound files, video files, Illustrator files, and other Flash SWF files. The import options will change depending on the type of file you have chosen.

To import files, select either [File] - [Import] from the menu or use the shortcut keys, [Ctrl]-[R]. When the Import dialog box appears, select the file to be imported and press the [Open] button. Importing sound and video files will be covered in more detail later in the book.

# Converting a Bitmap into a Vector Image

**Start File**

\Sample\Chapter02\02_007.fla

**Final File**

\Sample\Chapter02\02_007_end.fla

[1] Open the start file and select the dog image. Select [Modify] - [Bitmap] - [Trace Bitmap].

[2] When the Trace Bitmap dialog box appears, click [OK].

[3] The bitmap image has now been converted into a vector image.

## Let`s Go Pro!

**Start File**
- \Sample\Chapter02\image\telephone.psd

**Final File**
- \Sample\Chapter02\02_008_end.fla

# Importing Bitmap Images without a Background

The GIF and PNG image formats allow you to remove their backgrounds. This is known as transparency. Although these formats have this feature in common, there will be a difference in the image quality depending on which file format you choose. This example looks at these differences.

**01** The following image was made in Photoshop and has a transparent background. Two copies of the file have been saved, a GIF and a PNG file.

**02** Press [Ctrl]-[R] and hold down the [Ctrl] key as you click on the **telephone.gif** and **telephone.png** files. Press [Open] to import the files into Flash.

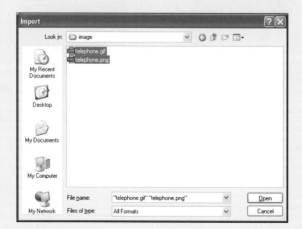

**03** The images will be imported on top of each other. Use the Selection tool to drag the top image to the right. Press [Ctrl]-[T] to open the Transform panel, then check the Constrain option. Set the width to 50 and press [Enter]. Select the remaining image and set it to 50% of the original width.

**04** You will be able to see that the images are transparent by adding a background color to the file. Click the stage and set the background color to #006699 in the Property Inspector.

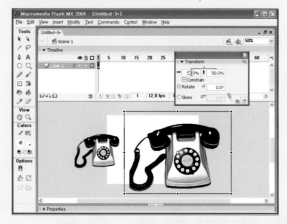

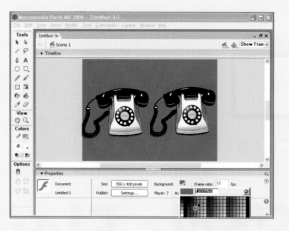

**05** Drag the images so that the GIF file is on the left and the PNG file is on the right. If you zoom into the GIF image, you will see that it is has jagged edges. Looking closely at the PNG image, you will notice that the edges are much smoother. Although the PNG format often looks superior, Web browsers don't support its usage as often as they do the GIF format. This is one of the reasons the GIF format is more widely used.

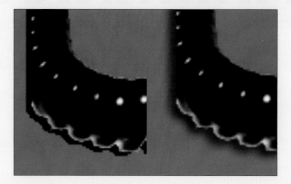

Chapter 3

# Basic Elements of Animation

Flash animations are created by playing a series of static images to give the effect of movement. This is the same effect that is created when flipping through a book with sequential drawings on each page. In this chapter, you will spend some time learning about the basic structure and elements of animating in Flash. These will include the timeline, the components of a timeline (frames and layers), and timeline effects. You will also learn to use symbols and the library.

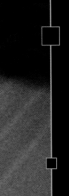

# Understanding the Basic Elements

The timeline, located just above the stage, is the primary tool with which you control animations in Flash. Since the idea behind the timeline is so important to animating in Flash, we will spend some time looking at the structure and elements of the timeline to make sure that you fully grasp the concepts before moving on.

## The Structure of the Timeline

Again, like films, the timeline could have tens, hundreds, or thousands of frames, depending on the length of the movie. Since you'll do most of your work in the timeline, refer to the following section to familiarize yourself with how it works.

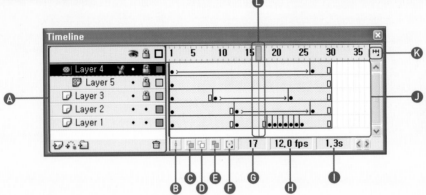

### Ⓐ Layers

You can think of layers as transparent sheets stacked on top of each other, as shown above. Other than the normal layers, you can insert guide layers, layer folders, and mask layers in the timeline. To keep the layers organized and easy to identify, give them descriptive names.

### Ⓑ Center Frame

Moves the frame marked by the playhead to the center of the timeline.

### Ⓒ Onion Skin

When this button is pressed, a Start Onion Skin marker and an End Onion Skin marker will appear around the playhead on the timeline. This function lets you view a few frames before and after the current frame. Only the contents of the current frame will appear as normal, the rest will look semi-transparent. Additionally, only the current frame can be edited.

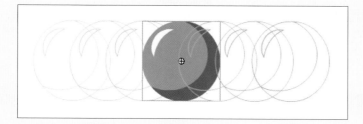

### ⓓ Onion Skin Outlines

This is the same as the Onion Skin command except that all frames but the current frame are displayed as outlines.

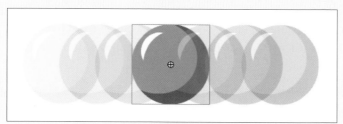

### ⓔ Edit Multiple Frames

When you use the Onion Skin feature, you can only select the object in the current frame. Turning on the Edit Multiple Frames feature, however, lets you edit the objects in other frames at the same time.

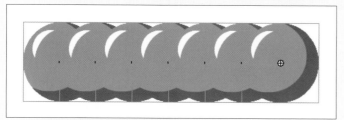

### ⓕ Modify Onion Markers

You can modify the onion markers in the following ways:

*Always Show Markers*: Always displays the onion skin markers on the timeline, regardless of whether onion skinning is turned on.

*Anchor Onion Markers*: Locks the markers to their current positions on the timeline so that they will not move with the playhead.

*Onion 2*: Shows two frames on either side of the current frame.

*Onion 5*: Shows five frames on either side of the current frame.

*Onion All*: All frames are shown.

### ⓖ Current Frame

Shows the frame currently displayed on the stage.

### ⓗ Frame Rate

This is the speed at which the animation is played. It is measured in number of frames per second (fps). Double-clicking on it opens the Document Properties dialog box where you can change the frame rate.

### ⓘ Elapsed Time

Refers to how long the animation has been playing in seconds.

### ❶ Frame

The frames in a layer are shown to the right of the layer name. Each frame contains a still image, and as these images are shown in sequence, the illusion of motion is created.

### ❷ Frame View Pop-Up menu

You can change the display of frames in the timeline by selecting from the options in the Frame View pop-up menu.

*Tiny, Small, Normal, Medium, Large*: These are width size options.

*Short*: For shortening the frames. When you have many layers, this option makes it possible for you to see more layers in the timeline.

*Tinted Frames*: Displays the frame sequences in different tints. For example, motion-tweened frames will be tinted in light blue on the timeline. The tint will not show up on the stage; it is only used to differentiate the frames in the timeline.

*Preview*: Shows a thumbnail of the objects in each frame (see below).

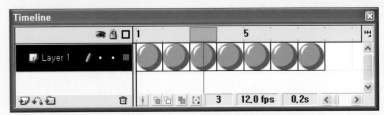

*1-5 Preview in Context*: Shows a thumbnail of the entire frame, including white space, so that you can see how the object changes position in the animation (see below).

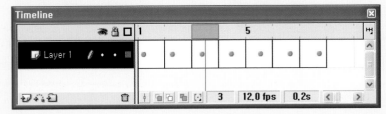

### ❸ Playhead

The playhead indicates the current frame that is being displayed on the stage. To display a frame on the stage, you can click-and-drag the playhead to the frame on the timeline.

tip >>

### Frame Rate

The default frame rate in Flash is 12 fps (frames per second). Flash animations are usually played on the Internet, which cannot handle the frame rates used for motion pictures (usually 24 or 30 fps). However, if the animation is preloaded (i.e., the animation is partially downloaded before a user plays it), the frame rate commonly used is 20 fps.

# Layers

If you have used graphics programs before, you will be familiar with layers. If you haven't, just think of layers as pieces of transparent cellophane that are stacked on top of one another. The images on the different layers are combined to create the final artwork.

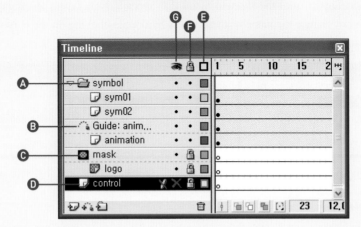

### Ⓐ Layer Folder

As you master more advanced Flash animation skills, the complexity of your work will grow. Eventually, you are likely to work on large projects, requiring the use of many layers. Chances are you will find it necessary to categorize the layers in order to work more efficiently. In this case, you can use layer folders to group similar layers into one folder. When you right-click on a layer folder, its shortcut menu will pop up and you can choose to apply the same options to all the layers in the folder. The options available let you show, hide, lock, or unlock other layers. You can also choose to show all layers in the folder as outlines.

### Ⓑ Motion Guide Layer

Using the Pen tool, you can draw the path along which your objects will move on the motion guide layer. Link the layer containing your objects to the motion guide layer to animate them along its path.

### Ⓒ Mask Layer

Mask layers are layers that display only certain areas of an object. You should first determine which area of the object should be displayed, then connect it to the layer below. Then, only the portions of the object specified by the mask layer will be shown.

### Ⓓ Current Layer

The current layer is the active layer on which you can draw or add objects. In the timeline, you will see a pencil icon next to the current layer.

### Ⓔ Show All Layers as Outlines

This icon allows us to view all of the layers in outlines. This menu contains sub-menus to further tailor the outline view.

### ❺ Lock/Unlock All Layers

Use this to lock or unlock the layers.

### ⑥ Show/Hide All Layers

Use this to display or hide the items on all the layers.

## Inserting Layers

By default, when you open a new document in Flash, it will contain a single frame on a single layer. We can add layers by selecting a layer and clicking on the [Add Layer] icon (🗐) in the timeline. We can also add layers by using the [Insert] - [Layer] command in the menu bar at the top, or by right-clicking on the layer and selecting [Insert Layer] from the shortcut menu that appears. New layers are always added above the selected layer. We can change the name of these layers by double-clicking on the current layer's name and typing in a new name.

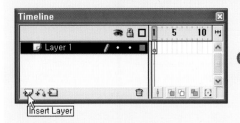 

## Moving Layers

Layers are stacked one on top of another, and their order can be rearranged as needed. To change the order of the layers, simply drag the layers to their desired positions.

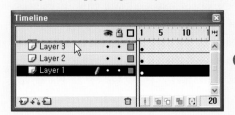 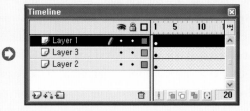

## Deleting Layers

Select the layer you want to delete from the timeline and click on the [Delete Layer] icon (🗑) to delete the layer. Another way of deleting layers is by right-clicking the layer and selecting [Delete Layer] from the shortcut menu that appears. To delete several layers at once, click on the layers you wish to delete one at a time while holding down the [Ctrl] key. Then, click on the [Delete Layer] icon (🗑).

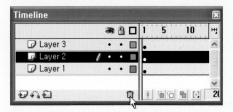

## Distributing Objects to Layers

The Distribute to Layers command takes the objects that are on one layer and distributes them to separate, new layers. This is useful when you want to animate the objects. First, select all the objects in the layer and right-click. To distribute the objects, select [Distribute to Layers] from the shortcut menu that appears. Objects can be distributed according to shape, group, text line, bitmap, or symbol.

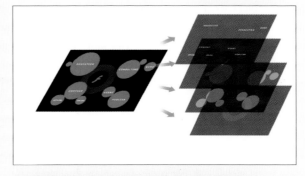

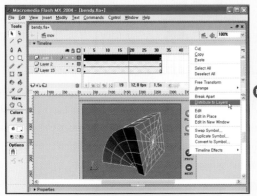

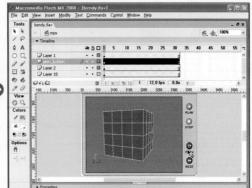

## Frames and Keyframes

When you open a new document, you will see a single layer containing a frame (marked with a circle) in the timeline. To the right of this frame are dimmed cells. To use a cell, you have to turn it into a frame, a keyframe, or an empty keyframe.

## Definition

There are two main categories of frames: frames and keyframes. When you add content to a frame, you will automatically turn it into a keyframe. Keyframes, which are marked on the timeline with a small black circle, are editable—frames are not. Frames are either empty or, if they are in the middle of two keyframes, contain content interpolated from the keyframes to create animation steps that fall between the keyframe reference points. In other words, frames only offer a preview of the animation's status between keyframes. As they are only previews, their content cannot be edited. Keyframes that do not contain any content are called empty keyframes and are indicated by an empty circle.

# Adding Frames or Keyframes

First, select where you want to insert a frame. Then, select [Insert] - [Timeline] - [Frame] or [Insert] - [Timeline] - [Keyframe] from the menu bar at the top. Another way to insert frames or keyframes is to right-click on the cell or frame where you want to insert them and select [Insert Frame] or [Insert Keyframe] from the shortcut menu when it appears.

# Removing Frames and Clearing Keyframes

When a frame is removed, the entire frame is deleted, reducing the total number of frames you have on the layer. On the other hand, when you clear a keyframe, you only remove the keyframe property and return the frame back to normal. The total number of frames in the timeline will remain unchanged.

# Moving Frames and Keyframes

In the timeline, click on the frame or keyframe you wish to move and drag it to a new location.

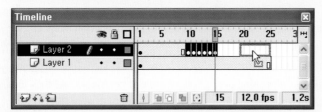

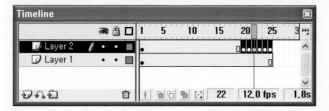

# Copying Frames and Keyframes

With the [Alt] key pressed down, click on the frame or keyframe you wish to copy and drag it to the desired location to make a copy. Alternatively, click on the frame you wish to copy and select [Edit] - [Timeline] - [Copy Frames] from the menu bar at the top. Then, click on the new location and select [Edit] - [Timeline] - [Paste Frames] from the menu bar to make a copy.

## Shortcut Menus and Shortcut Keys for Frames

You can right-click on any frame to open the shortcut menu for that particular frame. The menu contains commands that can be applied to the selected frame. To work fast, it is a good idea to memorize the shortcut keys for these commands.

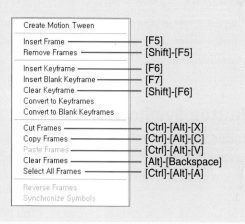

| Create Motion Tween | |
|---|---|
| Insert Frame | [F5] |
| Remove Frames | [Shift]-[F5] |
| Insert Keyframe | [F6] |
| Insert Blank Keyframe | [F7] |
| Clear Keyframe | [Shift]-[F6] |
| Convert to Keyframes | |
| Convert to Blank Keyframes | |
| Cut Frames | [Ctrl]-[Alt]-[X] |
| Copy Frames | [Ctrl]-[Alt]-[C] |
| Paste Frames | [Ctrl]-[Alt]-[V] |
| Clear Frames | [Alt]-[Backspace] |
| Select All Frames | [Ctrl]-[Alt]-[A] |
| Reverse Frames | |
| Synchronize Symbols | |

Symbols are special objects that you can create in Flash, and they provide one of the biggest advantages when it comes to keeping down the size of your Flash movies. Flash stores every object in your animation separately; even if the same objects are used repeatedly, each instance contributes to your final file size. By converting objects into symbols, you allow Flash to store a single "master" object that can be used repeatedly without increasing your file size. Any time you use an object more than once, you should be working with symbols.

You can turn an existing object into a symbol, or you can create a new, empty symbol that you can draw from scratch. It is normally easier to create a symbol from an existing object. All symbols for the movie are stored in the library and can be dragged onto the stage when needed. Dragging a copy of a symbol to the stage is called, "creating an instance," of the symbol. You can change instance properties such as color, size, and position without affecting the library copy.

Flash works with three types of symbols—graphics, buttons, and movie clips. In this section, we will learn more about how to work with graphic and button symbols. We will also learn a little about the library.

## Graphic Symbols

Graphic symbols are used as images within a movie. These are images that you want to use more than once. Graphic symbols are often used in simple animations, such as adding motion to an object using the motion-tween function.

## Button Symbols

Button symbols are symbols that are made to react to the mouse, and they are used often to make menus and navigation. Button symbols have their own timeline that looks different from the main timeline. Instead of numbered frames, the timeline for button symbols contains four frames—Up, Over, Down, and Hit.

The Up frame is the normal appearance when the mouse is not pointing at the button. The Over frame is the appearance when the mouse rests on or moves over the button. The Down frame shows what happens when the user holds down the mouse button or clicks. Finally, the Hit frame shows which part of the button is clickable.

## Movie Clip Symbols

A movie clip is a symbol with its own timeline. It allows you to create an animation that is independent of anything happening on the main timeline.

## Creating a New Symbol

To create a new symbol, select [Insert] - [New Symbol] from the menu bar or hit [Ctrl]-[F8]. In the Create New Symbol dialog box, give the symbol a name, select a symbol type, and click [OK].

## Converting an Existing Image to a Symbol

The Convert to Symbol dialog box is used to create a symbol from an image. Open this dialog box by selecting [Modify] - [Convert to Symbol] or by using the shortcut key, [F8]. You can enter the following information.

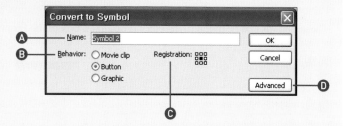

### Ⓐ Name

The name is used to reference the symbol in the library. It is important to select a meaningful name so that you can find your symbol easily.

### Ⓑ Behavior

The behavior selects the type of symbol to create.

### Ⓒ Registration

The registration point is used by Flash when symbols are positioned and transformed during an animation. The animation effects can change significantly depending on where the registration point is located within a symbol.

### Ⓓ [Advanced] Button

The [Advanced] button reveals additional options at the bottom of the dialog box. These options allow you to add an update feature for symbols that will be shared as part of a project. The Linkage area allows programmers to use the symbol in ActionScripting. When the Advanced section is open, the button changes to [Basic].

## Editing a Symbol

Editing a symbol is useful if you need to modify the symbol's appearance. You will also need to edit blank symbols to add content to them. When you edit a symbol, any copies or instances that are on the stage will also change.

To edit a symbol, right-click it and select [Edit] from the shortcut menu that appears. You can also display the library by selecting [Window] - [Library], right-clicking the symbol name, and choosing [Edit]. The symbol will then appear in editing mode. You will notice that the timeline title includes the name of the symbol being edited, and that you are no longer working on the stage.

You can make changes to your symbol using the drawing tools. When you have finished, click [Scene 1] at the top of the timeline to return to the stage. Any instances of the symbol should reflect the changes you made.

# Symbol Instance Properties

Each time you add a symbol instance to the stage, you can change properties such as brightness, tint, and alpha. These options can be found in the color drop-down box of the Properties panel when an instance is selected.

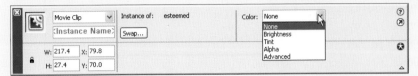

**Brightness** deals with the amount of white or black in an instance. It is a little like camera exposure. A normal instance has a brightness value of 0%. As you increase the value towards 100% the instance becomes whiter and whiter. It will be completely white at a setting of 100%. Reducing brightness below 0% adds black to the image, until it is totally black at -100%.

**Tint** adds a color on top of the existing instance. To use this setting, you must first select a color and then choose the tint percentage. A tint of 100% will completely fill the instance with the new color. Lesser values will provide a shading effect.

The **alpha** property deals with the transparency of an instance. A value of 100% means that the instance is totally visible. Values less than 100% fade the instance until, at 0%, the instance is no longer visible. The alpha property is often used for fade-in and fade-out effects during an animation.

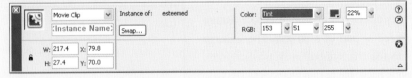

# The Library

The library contains all of the symbols that have been created within a movie. It may also contain sounds, video, and bitmap graphics. You can view the library by using the [Ctrl]-[L] shortcut keys or by selecting [Window] - [Library].

You can add a symbol to the stage by dragging it from the Library window. You can also organize your library contents into folders.

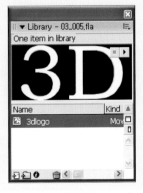

## Understanding Movie Clip Symbols

**Example File**
\Sample\Chapter03\03_005.fla

**❶** When you open the example file, you will see the words 3D Digital Studio in frame 1 of the timeline. Press [Ctrl]-[L] to open the library. The 3dlogo object is registered as a movie clip symbol. The text on the stage is an instance of the 3dlogo movie clip symbol.

**❷** Press [Ctrl]-[Enter] to test the movie. Even though the movie clip takes up only one frame in the main timeline, the 3D logo will be animated on the stage. This is because the movie clip is running on its own timeline.

**❸** Double-click the 3dlogo movie clip instance to view the symbol in Symbol Edit mode. If you look at the timeline for the movie clip, you will see that the 3D text is animated using frame-by-frame animation. This animation is completely independent of the main timeline.

## Understanding Timeline Effects

Timeline effects are new features within Flash MX 2004 that allow you to create simple animations with a single mouse click. Normally, the process of creating animations involves working with objects over many frames and layers. However, this has been greatly simplified with timeline effects. Creating an animation can be as simple as entering settings into a Timeline Effects dialog box.

# Blur Timeline Effect

The Blur effect creates and animates semi-transparent copies of an object to give the effect of a motion blur. The effect can be added by selecting [Insert] - [Timeline Effects] - [Effects] - [Blur] or by right-clicking an object to bring up its shortcut menu.

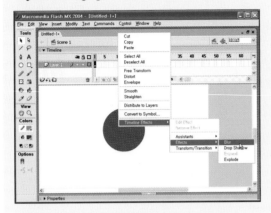

Final Animation

## The Blur Dialog Box

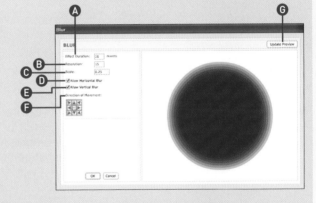

**A** **Effect Duration**: The length of the effect in frames. The higher this number, the longer the animation will take to complete.

**B** **Resolution**: The total number of blurred objects.

**C** **Scale**: The width of the blurred objects. The lower the number, the wider the visible border of the blurred objects.

**D** **Allow Horizontal Blur**: The blur effect is applied horizontally.

**E** **Allow Vertical Blur**: The blur effect is applied vertically.

**F** **Direction of Movement**: The direction in which the animation will move. Selecting the square in the center of the grid distributes the effect evenly about the selected shapes.

**G** **Update Preview**: Each time you enter Timeline Effect settings, you will need to click the [Update Preview] button to see the effect.

# Explode Timeline Effect

The Explode timeline effect creates an animation in which the object seems to explode on the stage.

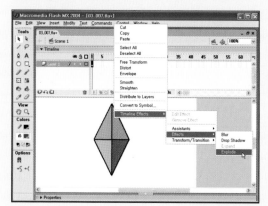

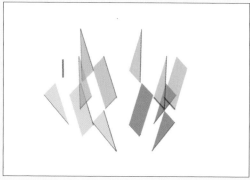

Explode Effect

## The Explode Dialog Box

**Ⓐ Effect Duration**: Length of the effect in frames.

**Ⓑ Direction of Explosion**: Direction in which the pieces are thrown during the explosion.

**Ⓒ Arc Size (x, y)**: Distance that the exploded pieces are thrown in pixels.

**Ⓓ Rotate Fragments by**: Rotation of fragments during explosion, in degrees.

**Ⓔ Change Fragments Size by (x, y)**: Change in size of fragments during explosion, in pixels.

**Ⓕ Final Alpha**: Final transparency setting in percentage.

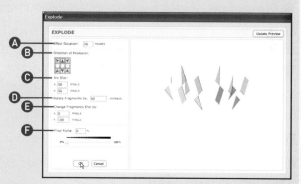

# Transform Timeline Effect

The Transform timeline effect can be used to apply movement and scaling animations to shapes.

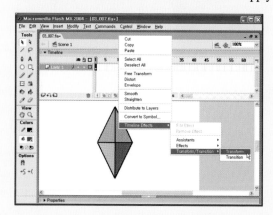

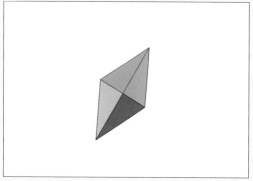

Final Animation

**A Effect Duration**: The length of the effect in frames.

**B Move to Position (x, y)**: The pixel co-ordinates to move to by the end of the effect.

**C Change Position by (x, y)**: The number of pixels to move by during effect; left-right and/or up-down.

**D Scale**: Percentage change in size.

**E Lock**: Scale both width and height using the same percentage value .

**F Unlock**: Apply different percentage scale settings to width and height.

**G Rotate**: Rotation during the effect, in degrees.

**H Spin**: The number of times to spin. Select clockwise or counterclockwise.

**I Change Color**: Check this option to include a color change.

**J Final Alpha**: Final transparency in percentage.

**K Final Color**: Color at the end of the animation if a color change is included.

**L Motion Ease**: From -100 to 100; eases motion from slow at the start to slow at the end of the animation.

# Transition Timeline Effect

The Transition timeline effect can be used to animate the introduction or exit of an object from the stage using wiping and fading effects.

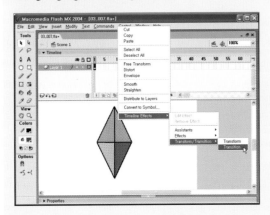

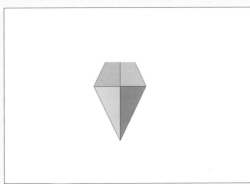

Final Animation

### The Transition Dialog Box

**A Effect Duration**: The length of the effect in frames.

**B Direction**: The In setting makes shapes appear during animation. The Out setting makes shapes disappear during animation.

**C Fade**: Animation uses a fade in or out.

**D Wipe**: Animation wipes in or out.

**E Motion Ease**: From -100 to 100; eases motion from slow at the start to slow at the end of the animation.

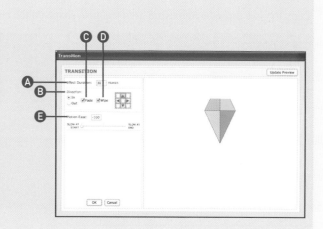

# Drop Shadow Timeline Effect

The Drop Shadow effect applies a shadow to the selected object.

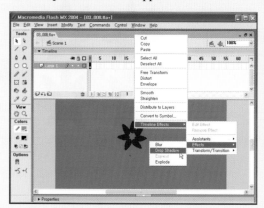

### The Drop Shadow Dialog Box

**A Color**: The color of the shadow.

**B Alpha Transparency**: The transparency of the shadow in percentage.

**C Shadow Offset**: The distance of the shadow from the shape in pixels.

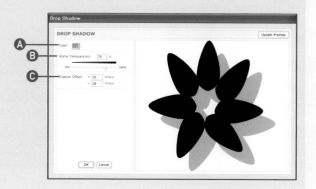

# Copy to Grid Timeline Effect

Copy to Grid is used to duplicate and arrange a shape on the stage.

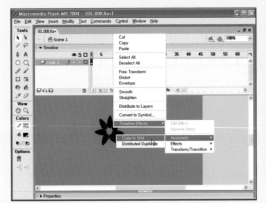

## Copy to Grid Timeline Effect

**Ⓐ Grid Size**

*Rows*: The number of rows of shapes to display.

*Columns*: The number of columns of shapes to display.

**Ⓑ Grid Spacing**

*Rows*: The distance between each row in pixels.

*Columns*: The distance between each column in pixels.

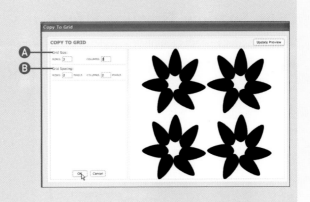

# Distributed Duplicate Timeline Effect

The Distributed Duplicated effect allows you to create and modify duplicates of your shape on the stage.

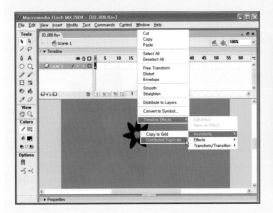

### The Distributed Duplicate Dialog Box

**Ⓐ Number of Copies**: The number of copies to create.

**Ⓑ Offset Distance**:

   *x*: The distance between copies, from left to right, in pixels.

   *y*: The distance between copies, from top to bottom, in pixels.

**Ⓒ Offset Rotation**: The number of degrees to rotate each copy.

**Ⓓ Offset Start Frame**: The number of frames between the appearance of each copy.

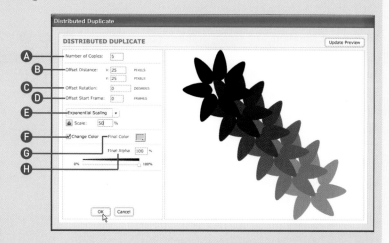

**Ⓔ Exponential/Linear Scaling**: Click the Lock button for different x and y settings. Changes the size by a percentage.

**Ⓕ Change Color**: Check to include a color change when duplicating.

**Ⓖ Final Color**: The color of the last copy.

**Ⓗ Final Alpha**: Transparency in percentage.

# Expand Timeline Effect

The Expand effect expands or contracts text.

## The Expand Dialog Box

**(A) Expand Duration**: The length of the effect in frames.

**(B) Expand**: Animation expands the letters.

**(C) Squeeze**: Animation starts expanded and squeezes letters together.

**(D) Both**: Animation squeezes them together.

**(E) Expand Direction**: The direction for the animation.

**(F) Shift Group Center by**: The amount in pixels that the center of the group is moved.

**(G) Fragment Offset**: The space between each element.

**(H) Change Fragment Size**: The change in size of each fragment in pixels.

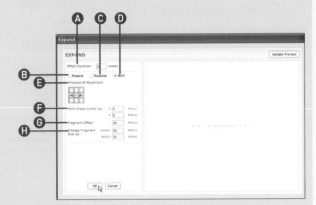

# Working with Frames

A lot of the work that you will do in Flash involves using frames, so it is important to develop your frame manipulation skills from the beginning. This exercise helps you work with frames and encourages you to use the shortcut menu and shortcut keys to work more efficiently. You'll also learn to insert a movie clip into your Flash file.

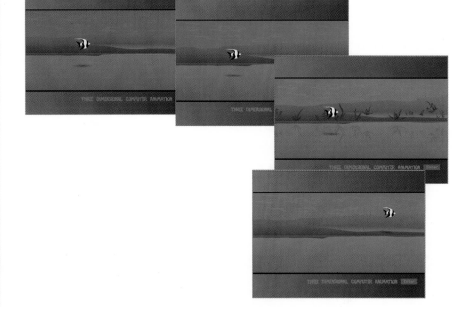

> **Start File**
> • \Sample\Chapter03\03_001.fla

> **Final File**
> • \Sample\Chapter03\03_001_end.fla

tip >>

**Selecting Several Frames at the Same Time – Method 1**

- If the frames to be selected are next to each other, either vertically or horizontally, hold down the [Shift] key and select the first and last frames. All the frames in between will be selected.
- To select a block of continuous frames, select a frame from one corner of the block. Hold down the [Shift] key and select a frame from the opposite corner.

1 Open the **Sample\Chapter03\ 03_001.fla** file from the supplementary CD. If you don't have the font used in this movie, a Missing Font Warning dialog box will appear. Click the [Use Default] button to replace the missing font with the default font.

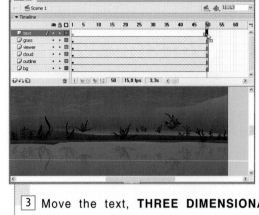

2 You will need to add frames 2 through 50 to all the layers. Click frame 50 of the text layer to select it. Hold down the [Shift] key and click on frame 50 of the bg layer. Right-click and select [Insert Frame] from the shortcut menu.

3 Move the text, **THREE DIMENSIONAL COMPUTER ANIMATION**, to frame 50 so that it appears briefly before the animation ends. Click on the first frame of the text layer and drag it to frame 50.

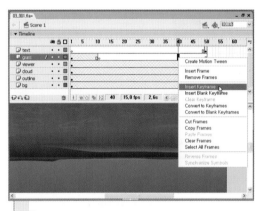

4 Alter the movie to make the plants along the river's edge disappear in the middle of the animation, and appear again towards the end. Right-click on frame 11 of the grass layer and select [Insert Blank Keyframe] from the shortcut menu. This will remove the content on frame 11 and all subsequent frames. If you had used the [Clear Frames] command, only the content on the selected frame would have been removed.

5 To make the plants appear again, right-click on frame 40 and select [Insert Keyframe].

6 Right-click on frame 1 and select [Copy Frames].

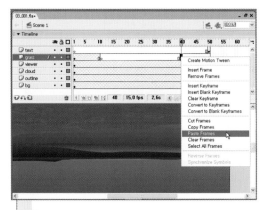

**tip >>**

## Selecting Several Frames at the Same Time – Method 2

- Another way of selecting continuous frames is to click on a frame and, without releasing the mouse, drag the cursor across all of the frames to be selected.
- If the frames are not next to each other, select the first frame or group of frames, hold down the [Ctrl] key, and select the next frame to add to the selection. You can continue to add frames by holding down the [Ctrl] key and clicking additional frames. If you select the wrong frame, clicking the [Ctrl] key again will clear the selection.

7 Right-click on frame 40 and select [Paste Frames]. The plants will appear from frame 40 onwards.

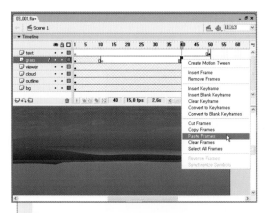

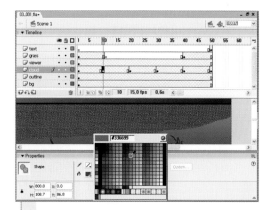

8 In this step, we will animate the sky by making the color change gradually as the movie runs. Start by inserting a keyframe at every tenth frame. Select frame 50 of the cloud layer and, holding down the [Ctrl] key, select frames 40, 30, 20, and 10. Press [F6] to insert keyframes.

9 Select frame 10 of the cloud layer and click on the sky on the stage. Check that you selected the sky and not the clouds. You should see a [Shape] icon in the Property Inspector. Click on the fill color box in the Property Inspector. When the color pop-up window appears, type **#336699** in the text box to color the sky cobalt blue. Repeat the step on the other keyframes using the following color values. Frame 20: **#666699**, Frame 30: **#805580**, Frame 40: **#267373**, Frame 50: **#496085**.

**tip >>**

## Using the [Ctrl] Key

In step 7, if you had selected the frames starting from frame 10 and ending with frame 50, you would have deselected all the frames when you clicked on frame 50. This is because you would have been holding down the [Ctrl] key when you selected frame 50, an ending keyframe. When you hold down the [Ctrl] key and move your mouse pointer over a starting or ending keyframe, it turns into a double-headed arrow, indicating that you can add or remove frames to the left or right of the keyframe.

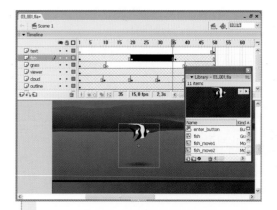

**10** We will now add another layer with a fish to the movie. Select the grass layer and click on the [Add Layer] icon ( ). Double-click on the name of the newly-added layer, type in **fish**, and press [Enter]. Press [Ctrl]-[L] to open the Library panel. Drag the fish_move1 movie clip to the stage, as shown.

**11** Insert a second movie clip showing the same fish swimming in a different style. Select frames 20 to 35 of the fish layer. Right-click and select [Clear Frames] from the shortcut menu to delete the content between these frames. Drag the fish_move2 movie clip from the Library panel to the upper, far-right of the stage.

**12** To test your movie, press [Ctrl]-[Enter]. This will open a new window. Close it to return to your movie.

# Managing Layer Folders

It is common to work on files that have over 100 layers for a single Flash animation. With that many layers, it's important to be organized and it makes sense to group layers together into folders. You can treat layer folders in the same way as individual layers. Each time you make a change to a folder, the change is applied to every layer inside the folder.

**Start File**

\Sample\Chapter03\03_002.fla

1 When you open the resource file, you should see an image of trees with the phrases, **Blue Day and Everybody has blue days.** Select the text Blue Day, right-click, and select [Break Apart] from the shortcut menu that appears.

2 Select all the objects on Layer 1 using [Ctrl]-[A]. Right-click and select [Distribute to Layers] from the pop-up menu.

**tip >>**

Applying the Break Apart command once to the text will break up the words into individual letters, while applying the command twice will turn the text into lines and fills.

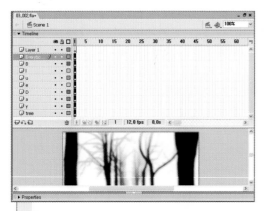

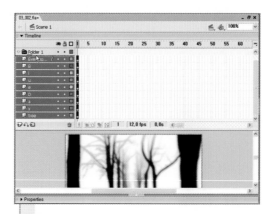

3 All of the objects will be distributed to separate layers. You can see that each of the letters in **Blue Day** has been placed onto its own layer. Notice that text layers use the letter they contain as their name, whereas layers containing other elements such as graphic objects will be named in numerical sequence (e.g., Layer 4).

4 The timeline looks cluttered with so many layers. Let's organize the layers with layer folders. Select the Everybo... layer and click on the [Insert Layer Folder] icon ().

5 Click the Everybo... layer and, holding down the [Shift] key, click on the bottommost layer to select all nine layers at the same time. Drag all nine layers to the new layer folder.

6 Click on the triangle icon (▷) next to the folder to close it. As you can see, packing the nine layers into the layer folder frees up a lot of space on the timeline. Next, move your cursor over the bottom edge of the timeline. When your pointer turns into a double-arrow symbol, click-and-drag the edge up to give more space to the stage.

7 Select frame 10 from the layer folder, right-click on this frame, and select [Insert Keyframe] from the pop-up menu that appears.

tip >>

### Moving Layers Inside Layer Folders

Layers in the layer folders are moved around in the same way as the layers outside the folders. You can also change their stacking order or move them out of the layer folder altogether.

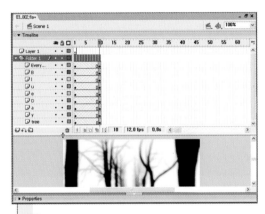

8 Click on the triangle icon (▷) to the left of the layer folder to open it. You can see that the [Insert Keyframe] command has been applied to all the layers in the folder.

9 Close the folder. This time select frame 30, right-click on this frame, and select [Insert Frame].

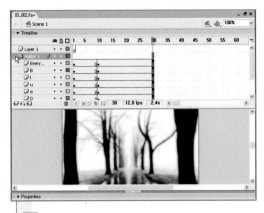

10 When you open the folder, you can see that the command has been applied to the same frame on all the layers in the folder. This is a quick way of applying the same command (Insert Frame, Delete Frame, Insert Keyframe, etc.) to all of the layers in a folder.

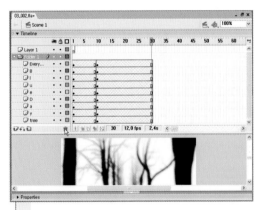

11 With the layer folder selected, click on the [Delete Layer] icon (🗑).

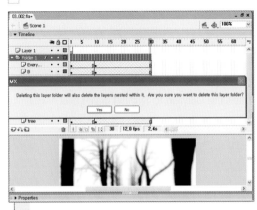

12 A warning message will appear, stating that by deleting the layer folder, you will also delete the layers within it. Click [Yes].

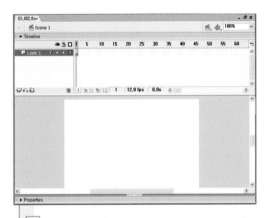

13 As shown above, deleting the layer folder will delete all the layers within the folder.

# 3

# Creating and Using Graphic Symbols

Symbols are the backbone of most of the animation that takes place within Flash. Whenever you use a graphic more than once, you should convert it to a symbol. This exercise helps you to create a graphic symbol and use instances of it on the stage.

**Start File**
● \Sample\Chapter03\03_003.fla

**Final File**
● \Sample\Chapter03\03_003_end.fla

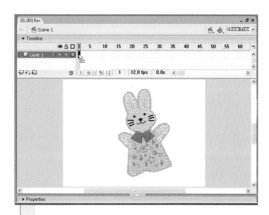

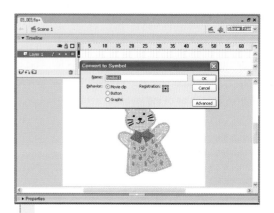

1 Open the start file and select frame 1 in Layer 1 in the timeline. You can see that all of the sections of the rabbit are selected on the stage.

2 Press [F8] to open the Convert to Symbol dialog box.

tip >>

## Convert to Symbol and Create New Symbol

- **Convert to Symbol**

Convert to Symbol is used to change an existing graphic into a symbol. This can be achieved by pressing [F8] or by selecting [Modify] - [Convert to Symbol]. The Convert to Symbol dialog box will display.

- **Create New Symbol**

To create an empty symbol, Press [Ctrl]-[F8] or select [Insert] - [New Symbol]. The Create New Symbol dialogue box will open.

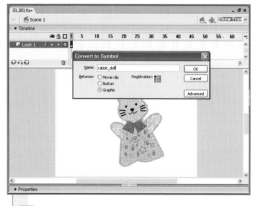

3  Enter **rabbit_doll** for the name, set the behavior to Graphic, and then click [OK]. When selected, the rabbit will be surrounded by a blue square and the Properties panel will display symbol properties.

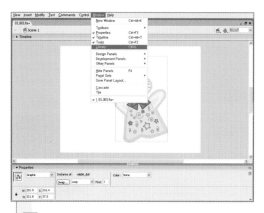

4  Select [Window] - [Library] to open the Library window.

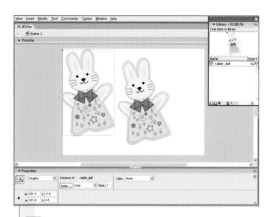

5  Drag another instance of the rabbit_doll symbol onto the stage from the Library window.

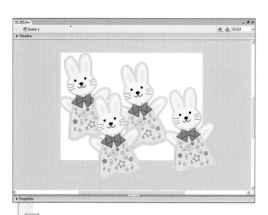

6  Repeat step 5 until you have four 'rabbit_doll' instances on the stage.

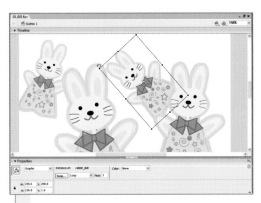

7  Use the Free Transform tool (⊞) to resize and rotate each of the instances differently.

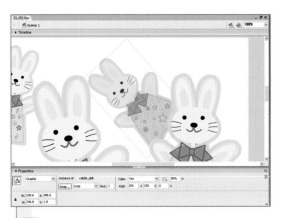

8  Select one of the 'rabbit_doll' instances and view the Properties panel. Change the color setting to Tint, select the tint color, and change the tint value to 30%.

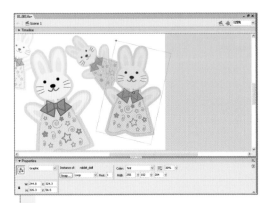

9  The instance should now appear with a different color.

10  Select another of the 'rabbit_ doll' instances and change the color property to Alpha. Set the alpha value to 50%.

11  Press [Ctrl]-[Enter] to test the movie. When you have finished, you will need to close this window to return to your Flash movie.

# 4 Creating Button Symbols

Button symbols are used to create interactivity with the mouse. Button symbols have their own timelines based on how the mouse is being used. Exercise 4 looks at the creation of button symbols.

**Start File**
  \Sample\Chapter03\03_004.fla

**Final File**
  \Sample\Chapter03\03_004_end.fla

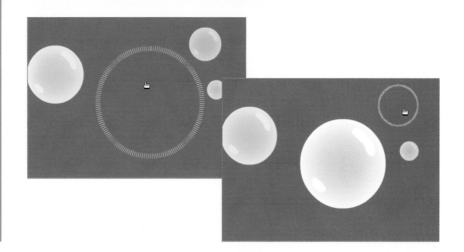

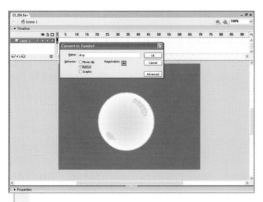

1 Open the start file and select frame 1 in Layer 1 on the timeline. Press [F8] to open the Convert to Symbol dialog box. Enter **drop** for the name, set the behavior to Button, and then click [OK].

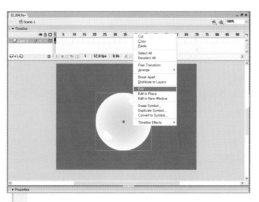

2 Right-click the mouse on the symbol on the stage and select [Edit] from the shortcut menu that appears.

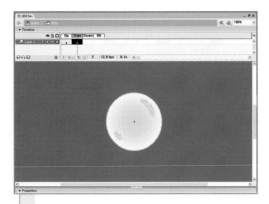

3 We are now editing the button. Notice that there are four frames in the timeline. Select the Over frame and press [F6] to create a keyframe.

4 With the playhead on the Over frame, remove the surfaces of the object with the Arrow tool. Double-click on the line, set the line thickness to 10 pt in the Properties panel, and change the style to a hatched line.

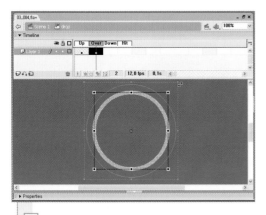

5 Select the Free Transform tool and click the circle, making sure you are still in the Over frame of the timeline.

Hold down the [Shift]-[Alt] keys. Drag to increase the size of the circle.

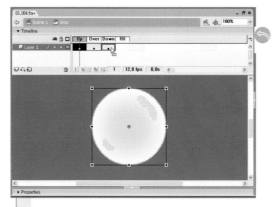

6 Select the Up frame. Hold down the [Alt] key and drag it to the Down frame.

tip >>

When you drag a corner with the Free Transform tool, holding down the [Shift] key constrains the shape to a perfect square or circle. Using the [Alt] key centers the shape.

tip >>

**Copying Keyframes**

You can also select [Control] - [Test Movie] from the menu to preview the movie in the Test Movie window.

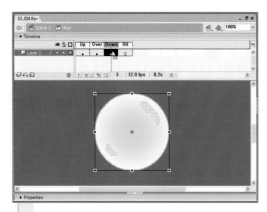

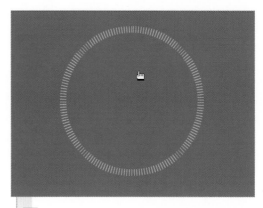

**7** Select the Down frame, press [F5], and insert a frame into the Hit frame. This tells Flash to set the clickable area of the button to the area in the Down frame.

**8** Press [Ctrl]-[Enter] to test the movie. Point to the button and click it. Watch how the button changes in response to your mouse movement.

### note >>
### Test Movie Window

The library contains all the symbols that are used in the movie. You can use it to search for symbols that don't appear on the stage. If the symbol is already on the stage, you can duplicate it by copying and pasting or by dragging with the [Alt] key held down.

### tip >>
### Test Movie Window

You can copy keyframes by clicking and dragging with the [Alt] key held down. A + sign appears on the mouse pointer to let you know that the keyframe is being duplicated.

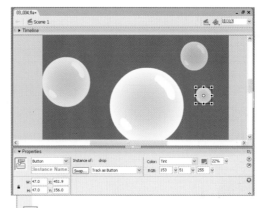

**9** Close the Test Movie window and return to the Symbol Editing screen. Click on [Scene 1] in the timeline to return to the stage. Click and hold on the 'drop' button symbol with the [Alt] key held down. Drag the mouse to create a new instance of the symbol. Change the size and position of the copied symbol as shown and add a tint.

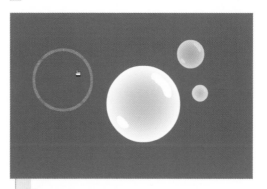

**10** Press [Ctrl]-[Enter] to test the movie.

# 5 Creating Blur Timeline Effect

In this exercise, you will learn to create the Blur timeline effect. You will also learn to edit and remove this effect from your animation.

**Final File**
- \Sample\Chapter03
  \03_006_01_end.fla

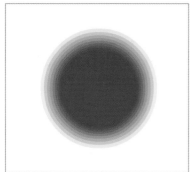

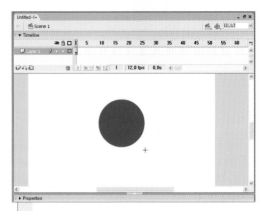

1 Select [File] - [New] or click [Create New] - [Flash Document] from the start page to open a new movie. Click the Oval tool and select a red fill color. Clear the line color and hold down the [Shift] key while using the tool to draw a circle.

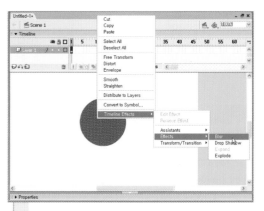

2 Right-click the circle and select [Timeline Effects] - [Effects] - [Blur] from the shortcut menu.

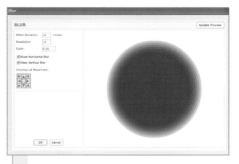

3 In the Blur dialog box, enter the following settings: Effect Duration: **20 frames**, Resolution: **10**, Scale: **0.5**. Click the [Update Preview] button to see the effect.

tip >>

## Direction of Movement

Use the arrow keys to determine the direction of movement within an animation. For example, click the arrow shown above and click the [Update Preview] button to see the following effect.

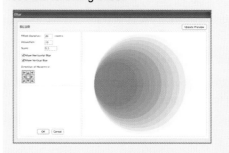

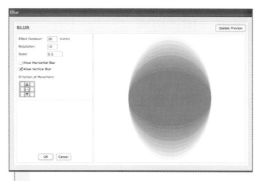

4 | Uncheck the Allow Horizontal Blur option. The left and right buttons will be removed from the Direction of Movement section. Press [Update Preview] to preview the animation in the Blur dialog box.

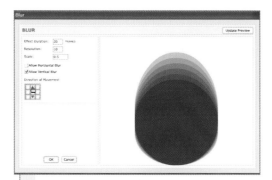

5 | Click the upward pointing arrow in the Direction of Movement option. Update the preview. The animation should show the object expanding at the top and then gradually disappearing. Press [OK] to add the timeline effect to the object on the stage.

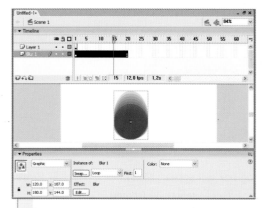

6 | Select the object on the stage. The Property Inspector shows that it is a graphic symbol. The timeline includes the Blur 1 layer made up of 20 frames.

7 | Press [Ctrl]-[L] to open the Library window. The Blur 1 symbol and the Effects folder have been added to the library. If you open this folder, you will see that it contains symbol 1.

8 | Press [Ctrl]-[Enter] to test the movie. Check to see that the Blur effect has been applied to your object.

# Editing the Blur Timeline Effect

**1** Right-click the circle symbol on the stage and select [Timeline Effects] - [Edit Effect] from the shortcut menu.

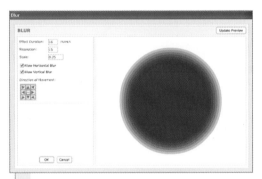

**2** The Blur dialog box will appear. Make the following changes: Effect Duration: **30 frames**, Resolution: **20**, Scale: **1**. Ensure that both the Allow Horizontal Blur and Allow Vertical Blur options are checked and click the center box in the Direction of Movement option. Click [OK] to apply the changes.

**3** Press [Ctrl]-[Enter] to test the movie.

# Editing Blur Animation on the Timeline

If you edit the frames within the animation on the timeline, you will no longer be able to update the timeline effect using the Blur dialog box.

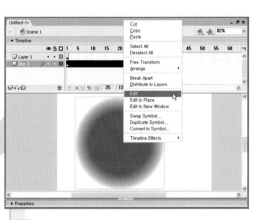

**1** Right-click the circle containing the timeline effect and select [Edit] from the shortcut menu.

tip >>

## Effect Setting Warning

This warning message will appear whenever you try to edit an object that has a timeline effect applied. Clicking [OK] will stop you from being able to modify the timeline effect using the Edit Effect command.

[2] You should see the Effect Settings Warning dialog box. Click [OK] to continue editing the object.

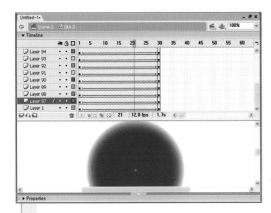

[3] When you edit the animation, the view will change to the Symbol Edit window. The layers and frames used to create the animation effect will be displayed.

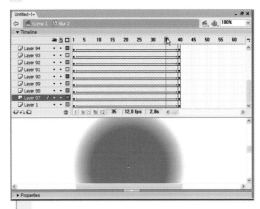

[4] Click frame 5 in the timeline and press [F5] to insert frames until you have a total of 40 frames.

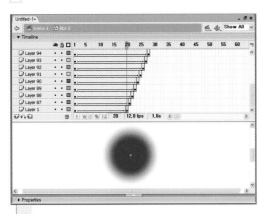

[5] Drag the mouse over everything from the top layer to the last keyframe and move one frame at a time. Selecting the remaining frames below the keyframe, press [Shift]-[F5] to delete.

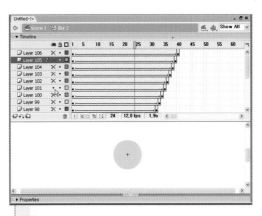

[6] Click one of the layer title on the left of the timeline. Click on the Show/Hide option while holding down the [Alt] key to hide all other layers.

7 Press [Ctrl]-[Enter] to test the movie. Check to see that the animation has been edited.

# Removing Blur Animation

**Start File**

\Sample\Chapter03\03_006.fla

**Final File**

\Sample\Chapter03\03_006_04_end.fla

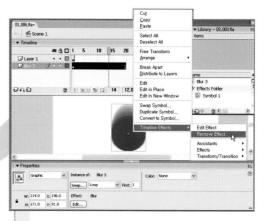

1 Open the start file and right-click the object on the stage. Select [Timeline Effects] - [Remove Effect] from the shortcut menu.

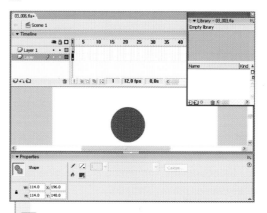

2 The Blur effect will be removed from the selected object. The object will change from a symbol to a shape, and animation frames will be removed from the timeline. If you view the library using [Ctrl]-[L], you will see that it has been cleared.

# Inserting Attention Grabbing Effects

The Explode, Transform, and Transition timeline effects are among the best showstoppers in Flash's list of timeline effects. All of these showy effects are sure to capture attention from your movie's viewers. In this exercise, let's learn to create the Explode, Transform, and Transition timeline effects to make the original object more dynamic.

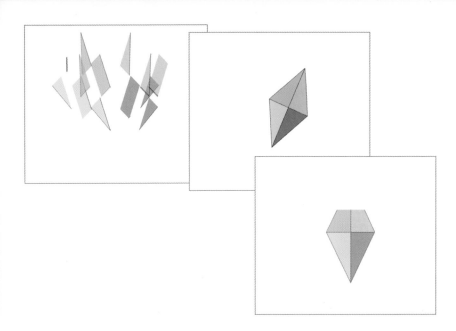

## Explode Timeline Effect

**Start File**
\Sample\Chapter03\03_007.fla

**Final File**
\Sample\Chapter03\03_007_01_end.fla

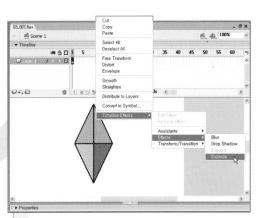

1 Click on [File] - [Open] to open the start file. Select all objects on the stage, right-click, and select [Timeline Effects] - [Effects] - [Explode].

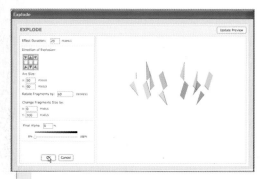

2 In the Explode dialog box, click on the center top arrow in the Direction of Explosion grid. Set the y-value of the [Change Fragments Size by] option to 100 pixels. Don't change any of the other settings and click [OK] to apply the effect.

3 Press [Ctrl]-[Enter] to preview the movie.

# Transform Timeline Effect

**Start File**
\Sample\Chapter03\03_007.fla

**Final File**
\Sample\Chapter03\03_007_02_end.fla

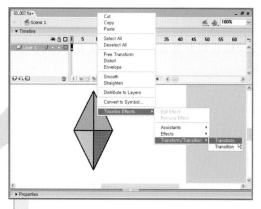

1 Open the start file, select all shapes, right-click, and choose [Timeline Effects] - [Transform/Transition] - [Transform].

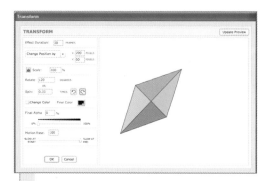

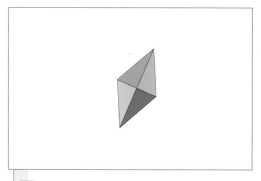

2 In the Transform dialog box, make the following changes to the settings: Change Position by: **200** (x), **50** (Y); Rotate: **120,** and Final Alpha: **0%**. Click [OK].

3 Press [Ctrl]-[Enter] to preview the results.

# Transition Timeline Effect

**Start File**
\Sample\Chapter03\03_007.fla

**Final File**
\Sample\Chapter03\03_007_03_end.fla

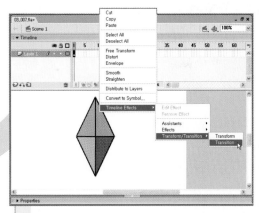

1 Open the start file, select all shapes, right-click, and choose [Timeline Effects] - [Transform/Transition] - [Transition].

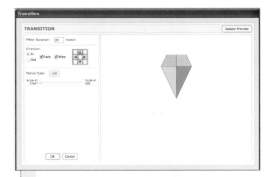

2 In the Transition dialog box, click on the top arrow in the direction grid and move the motion ease bar towards [slow at start] until the motion ease value changes to -100. You could also type in this value. Click [OK].

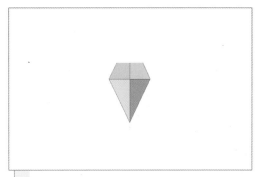

3 Press [Ctrl]-[Enter] to preview the results.

# Making Copies and Applying Timeline Effects

In this exercise, you will learn to use the Drop Shadow, Copy to Grid, and Distributed Duplicate timeline effects. Since all these timeline effects involve making one or more copies of an object and then moving them around, the exercises for each of these timeline effects are grouped into one exercise.

## Drop Shadow Timeline Effect

**Start File**
\Sample\Chapter03\03_008.fla

**Final File**
\Sample\Chapter03\03_008_01_end.fla

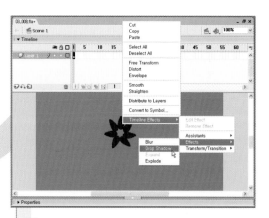

1 Open the start file, right-click the object, and select [Timeline Effects] - [Effects] - [Drop Shadow].

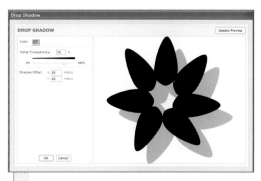

2 Without changing the settings in the Drop Shadow dialog box, click [OK].

3 Press [Ctrl]-[Enter] to preview the Drop Shadow effect.

# Copy to Grid Effect

**Start File**
\Sample\Chapter03\03_008.fla

**Final File**
\Sample\Chapter03\03_008_02_end.fla

1 Open the start file, right-click the shape, and select [Timeline Effects] - [Assistants] - [Copy to Grid] from the shortcut menu.

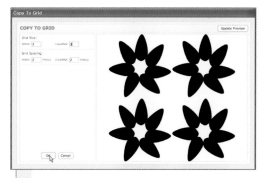

2 Set Rows to 3 and Columns to 3 in the Grid Size options. Click [OK] and the stage will contain nine duplicated shapes.

3 Press [Ctrl]-[Enter] to preview the Copy to Grid effect.

# Distribute Duplicated Effect

**Start File**
\Sample\Chapter03\03_008.fla

**Final File**
\Sample\Chapter03\03_008_03_end.fla

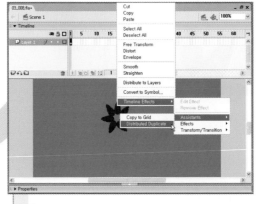

1 Open the start file, right-click the shape, and select [Timeline Effects] - [Assistants] - [Distributed Duplicate].

2 Change the settings in the Distributed Duplicate dialog box as follows: Scale: **50%**, and Final Color: **#FFFF00**. Click [Update Preview] to view the effect. Click [OK] to apply the effect and return to the stage.

3 Press [Ctrl]-[Enter] to preview the Distributed Duplicate effect.

# Using Timeline Effects to Create Text Animations

You can also apply timeline effects to text objects to create simple but effective text animations. These effects look best with short, large-sized text. In this exercise, you will use the Blur, Expand, and Explode timeline effects to animate a line of text.

## Blur Timeline Effect

**Start File**
\ Sample \ Chapter03 \ 03_009.fla

**Final File**
\ Sample \ Chapter03 \ 03_009_01_end.fla

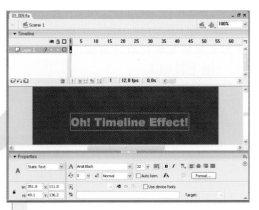

1 Click [File] - [Open] to open the start file. The Property Inspector will show that the object is a text object.

2 Right-click the text and choose [Timeline Effects] - [Effects] - [Blur].

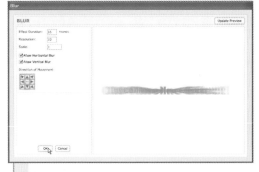

3 In the Blur dialog box, set the Resolution to 10, the Scale to 1, and click on the center arrow at the bottom for the Direction of Movement option. Click [OK] to apply the effect.

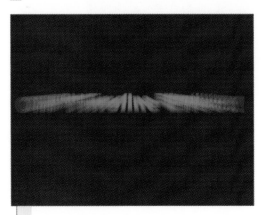

4 Press [Ctrl]-[Enter] to preview the results.

# Expand Timeline Effect

**Start File**
\Sample\Chapter03\03_009.fla

**Final File**
\Sample\Chapter03\03_009_02_end.fla

1 Click on [File] - [Open] to open the start file, right-click the shape, and select [Timeline Effects] - [Effects] - [Expand].

**2** In the Expand dialog box, select the Both radio button and set Change Fragment Size by to Height 50 and Width 50. Click [OK] to apply the effect.

**3** Press [Ctrl]-[Enter] to preview the results.

# Explode Timeline Effect

**Start File**
\Sample\Chapter03\03_009.fla

**Final File**
\Sample\Chapter03\03_009_03_end.fla

**1** Open the start file, right-click the text, and select [Timeline Effects] - [Effects] - [Explode].

**2** Enter the following settings: Rotate Fragments by: **180**, Change Fragments Size by: **100** (X), **100** (Y). Click [OK].

**3** Press [Ctrl]-[Enter] to test the movie.

Chapter | 4

# Animating in Flash

The word *animation* originated from the Latin word for soul, *anima*, and the word *animatus*, which means to move to action and give life to. In this chapter, we bring together everything you have learned in the preceding pages and let you put theory into practice. You will have fun creating your own animations in this chapter, which contains tutorials for frame-by-frame animation, motion-tweened animation, and animation using ActionScript.

# Animation Methods and Characteristics

Every frame in an animation contains a still image. As the frames play in quick succession, you get an illusion of movement. The more frames you have per second, the smoother the movement. There are three methods for animating in Flash: frame-by-frame animation, tweened animation, and animation using ActionScript.

## Frame-By-Frame Animation

Frame-by-frame animation is the most straightforward method for creating animations. As the name implies, you create the still images frame by frame. Another name for frame-by-frame animation is cell animation. This is an old method for producing animations for cinema, television, and computers. Although this technique is great for creating detailed animations, and gives you the most creative control, it is very laborious and time-consuming.

## Tweened Animation

In tweened animation, you create a starting keyframe and an ending keyframe and let Flash fill in the frames between. Flash automatically creates the in-between frames based on the images of the two keyframes. This is a much faster approach than frame-by-frame animation, where you have to create the frames one by one.

There are two types of tweened animation: shape tweening and motion tweening. Before you tween an animation, you have to specify the kind of tweening you are going to perform. First, select the frames you want to tween. Then select Motion or Shape from the Property Inspector.

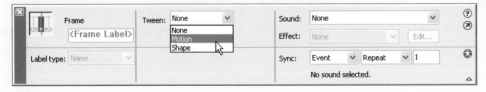

## Shape Tweening

You've probably seen examples of morphing effects in science fiction movies. Morphing is a common technique for showing transformations (a human changing into an animal, for instance) with the assistance of digital effects. Although you can't recreate the sophisticated 3D effects you see in the cinema with Flash, you can turn one object into another with shape tweening. You can tween shapes to change their size, shape, color, and position.

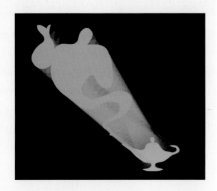

If shape tweening is applied correctly, the tweened frames in the timeline will be colored light green, and a solid arrow will appear between the keyframes. When there is a mistake, you will see a dotted arrow across the frames in the timeline.

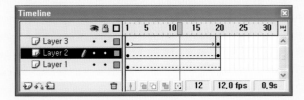

## Motion Tweening

In motion tweening, you can make an object move along a path you select. You can also change its properties by manipulating the object's ending frame. You can tween the position, size, and rotation for differnt instances, groups, and type. To tween the colors of groups or type, you must turn them into symbols first.

As with shape tweening, you will see a solid arrow across the tweened frames when the motion tweening is applied correctly. If you make such mistakes as omitting an ending keyframe, you will see a dotted arrow in the timeline.

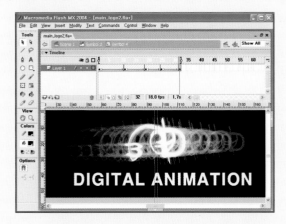

## Animation Using ActionScript

This final technique does not line up the frames to make the animation. Instead, it uses ActionScript–the scripting language of Flash—to control the movie. An advantage of scripting is that you can create the effects with a small file size. Because you will need to have a basic understanding of the ActionScript language, it will take more effort to master than tweening.

You will learn more about ActionScript in Chapter 5.

# Captivating Line Effects Using Frame-by-Frame Animation - A Rotating Earth

The animation we will be creating in this example changes the color of a different line in every frame so as to draw the viewer's gaze from the outside in. As animation techniques go, this is the most time-consuming of all, as you need to pay careful attention to detail. This example provides an excellent opportunity for you to review the concepts you have learned so far, and to gain a more concrete understanding of timelines, frames, and animation.

**Start File**
● \Sample\Chapter04\04_001.fla

**Final File**
● \Sample\Chapter04\04_001_end.fla

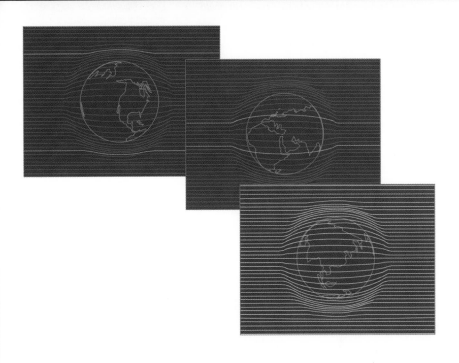

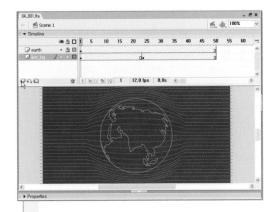

1 Select [File] - [Open] to open the resource file. Select the Earth layer and click on the [Add Layer] icon (⬛) to add a new layer.

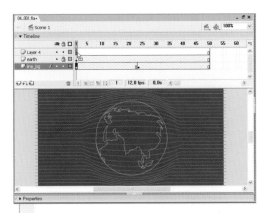

2 Select frame 1 of the line_bg layer. With the [Alt] key pressed down, drag it to the new layer to make a copy. After frame 1 is copied onto the new layer, the name of the layer changes to line_bg. Now you'll have two layers with the same name.

## Three Ways of Selecting Several Frames at Once

- If the frames you want to select are side by side, click on the first frame and then the last frame while holding down the [Shift] key.
- Another way is to click on the first frame and, without releasing the mouse, drag to the last frame.
- If the frames are not side by side, hold down the [Ctrl] key and click on the frames you want to select one at a time to add to the selection.

Which method you choose is a matter of personal preference.

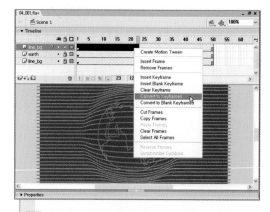

3 While holding down the [Alt] key, click on the [Lock/Unlock All Layers] icon (🔒) of the new line_bg layer to lock all of the other layers. Hold down the [Alt] key whenever you want to apply a layer option to all the layers except the selected one. Select frames 1 to 23 of the new line-bg layer, right-click, and select [Convert to Keyframes] from the pop-up menu. You can see from the timeline that the frames have been converted into keyframes.

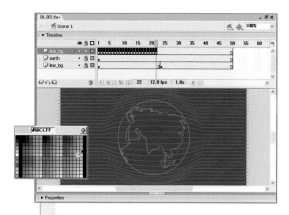

4 Select the Ink Bottle Tool (🍶) from the toolbox and set the line color to #66CCFF, as shown above.

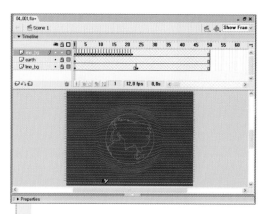

5 Notice that your cursor has turned into an Ink Bottle pointer. Select frame 1 and check that all the lines are deselected. Next, click on the topmost and bottommost lines to apply the color to these lines. When you are done, select frame 2 and click on the second topmost and bottommost lines to change their color.

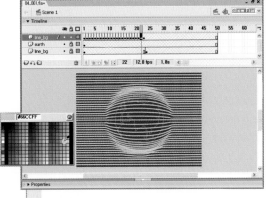

tip >>

**Undo and Redo**

The Undo command can be accessed by selecting [Edit] - [Undo] from the menu bar or by using the shortcut keys, [Ctrl]-[Z]. The Undo command can cancel up to 100 previous operations. If you cancel a step by mistake, you can recover it with the Redo command. To activate the Redo command, select [Edit] - [Redo] from the menu bar or hit the shortcut keys, [Ctrl]-[Y].

6   Repeat step 5 on all the frames. The objective is to change the color of the lines until you hit center. After a while, you may forget which line you were working on, so you may want to move the playhead from frame to frame to check your work.

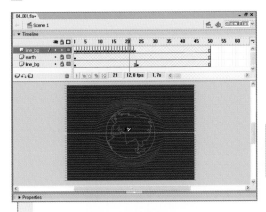

7   By the time you get to frame 21, you will have one line left. As in preceding steps, use the Ink Bottle tool ( ) on the final line to change the color.

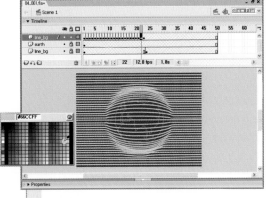

8   Change the window size to 50% from the top-right corner of the stage. Then select frame 22. With all of the lines on frame 22 selected, set the line color to #66CCFF.

tip >>

**Opening the Property Inspector**

Open the Property Inspector by selecting [Window] - [Properties] or by using the shortcut keys, [Ctrl]-[F3].

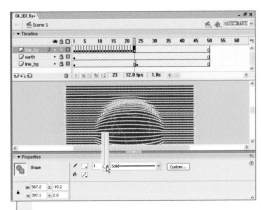

9   Select frame 23. With all of the lines on frame 23 selected, change the line color to white (#FFFFFF) and the line thickness to 1 in the Property Inspector.

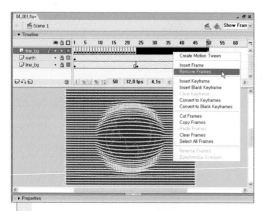

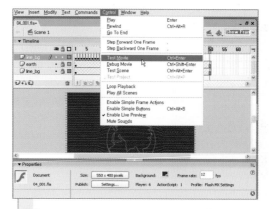

10 Select frames 24 to 50. Right-click and select [Remove Frames], or press [Shift]-[F5] to delete the selected frames.

11 Let's run a test. Select [Control] - [Test Movie] from the menu bar or press [Ctrl]-[Enter]. The test will show you how the SWF movie file will look when it is played. In addition, if the movie is uploaded onto the Internet, Test Movie also checks how long it takes to download the movie from the Web.

tip >>

## Make a Habit of Saving Your Work Periodically!

If you don't make a habit of saving your work periodically, you could lose everything in the event of a power failure or surge. Your computer could also crash, especially when working in a memory-intensive graphics program like Flash. These are the most common scenarios, but as you probably know, computers are unreliable machines, and you may lose your work in an instant. To avoid such painful incidents, get into the habit of periodically pressing [Ctrl]-[S] (the shortcut keys for Save) as you work.

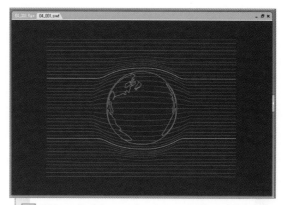

12 This animation grabs the attention of the viewer by focusing his gaze on the center of the converging lines. To end the test movie, close the test window and you will return to your Flash workspace. If you spotted some mistakes in the test, make the necessary corrections and test again.

**Start File**
\Sample\Chapter04\04_002.fla

**Final File**
\Sample\Chapter04\04_002_end.fla

# The Revolving Earth

This movie was created using frame-by-frame animation. You may be thinking that this would have involved drawing each and every frame to simulate the movement of the rotating earth. Well, yes and no. Animating frame by frame is time consuming and the resulting file size is huge. In this section, we will learn an easier way to work using frame-by-frame animation. For starters, remember that it's a good idea to plan beforehand so that you can create an animation efficiently and effectively.

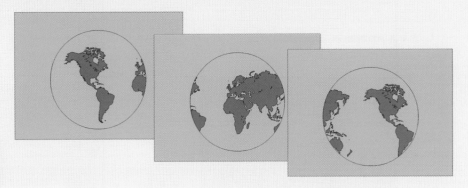

**01** First of all, open the example file to see how the movie was made. Press [Ctrl]-[O] and select the **04_001_end.fla** file from the \Sample\Chapter04 folder. Holding down the [Alt] key, click the [Lock/Unlock] icon (🔒) of the earth layer to lock all the other layers. On the stage, right-click on the globe and select [Edit] from the pop-up menu.

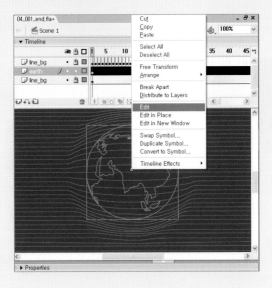

**02** Move the playhead from frame to frame and you will observe that every frame contains a different stage of the earth's rotation. If you were asked to create the rotation stages to fill all 23 frames, you'd probably close this book! But, don't worry, there is an easier way to get this done.

**03** If you open the resource file, you will see a flat, 2D image of the earth. We are going to add a mask layer to the earth so that only the area inside the circle is visible. To create a mask layer, add a new layer and name it **circle**. Then, lock the earth_plane layer.

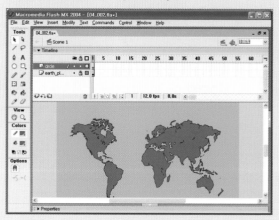

**04** Select the Oval tool (○) from the toolbox and draw a slightly larger circle on the map.

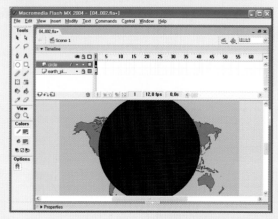

**05** Use the Arrow tool to select the circle and press [Shift]-[F9] to open the Color Mixer panel. To see the map area covered by the circle, set the alpha value to 0% and click on the stage. This will turn the circle transparent, as shown above.

tip >>
## What's a Mask?

In Flash, you can use a mask layer to hide and show selective portions of the image underneath it. For example, if you place a filled circle on a mask layer, the underlying layers will only show through the circle. Areas outside the circle are hidden.

In the globe tutorial, you have to make the flat, 2D map look like a globe. To do so, you must first place the map layer below the round globe layer. Then, we will apply a mask to the round globe layer so that only this rounded area is seen in the flat map layer underneath.

**06** Select the circle layer and press [Ctrl]-[F8] to open the Create New Symbol dialog box. Name the symbol **clarity_circle** and click [OK] to open the movie clip symbol-editing mode. Clicking on the Scene 1 clapper or the blue arrow (⇦) below the timeline will return you to the main stage.

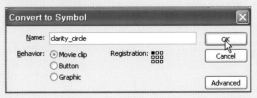

**note >>**

In the Create New Symbol dialog box, you can choose from three symbol behaviors: movie clip, button, and graphic. These three behaviors are types of symbols with distinct characteristics.

**tip >>**

## Why Do I Need to Register the Circle As a Symbol?

A symbol is a master copy of a graphic, button, or movie clip that is stored in the library. Once you turn an object into a symbol, it can be used over and over again. To use a symbol, you drag a copy called an instance from the master copy in the library. When you use symbols, you reduce the file size of your document. This is because Flash stores the symbol only once, regardless of how many instances you pull out. For example, even if you created 100 instances, the computer will only need to save one symbol rather than a hundred.

If you intend to play your Flash animation over the Web, a small file size is essential for speed. In addition, if you intend to use the same object more than once, it is a good idea to turn it into a symbol first. You will save a lot of time on editing as you will only need to edit the symbol and the instances will be updated automatically. In this example, we saved the circle as a symbol because we will be using it as a mask element and as the outline of the globe.

**07** Let's make a copy of the circle layer. First, add a new layer. Then, with frame 1 of the circle layer selected, hold down the [Alt] key and drag it to the first frame of the new layer. The new layer's name automatically changes to **circle**. This new circle layer will be used as an outline of the globe.

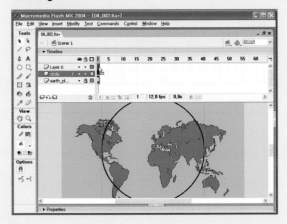

**08** Click the [Lock/Unlock] icon (🔒) of the earth_plane layer while holding down the [Alt] key to lock all the other layers. Double-click on the map to convert to editing mode, select frame 1, and press [Ctrl]-[G] to group all the objects on this layer together.

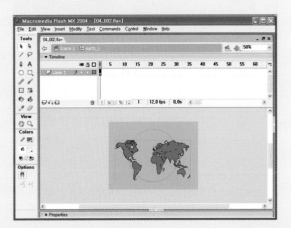

**09** With the map selected, hold down the [Ctrl] key and drag a copy out to one side. Check that the two images line up horizontally and the spacing between them is adequate.

**10** Click the Scene 1 clapper below the timeline or the blue arrow (⬅) to return to the main stage. Selecting the 30th frame on all the layers, press [F5] to insert frames. Next, select only frame 30 of the earth_plane layer and press [F6] to insert a keyframe.

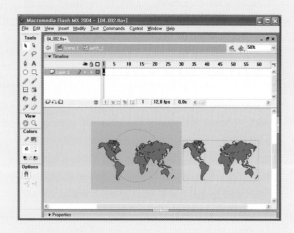

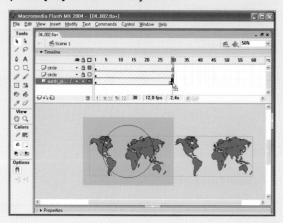

**11** Moving the playhead to frame 1, position the map face-to-face with the circle—which acts as the globe outline—on the stage. See the figure below.

**12** Move the playhead to frame 30 and move the map to the left of the stage. Move the image of the map so that its right side lines up with the left side of the map in frame 1.

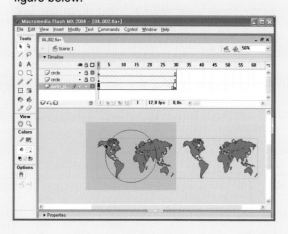

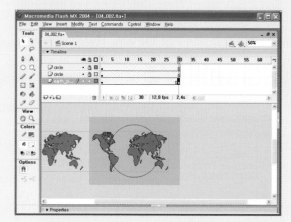

**13** Right-click on any frame (between 1 and 29) from the earth_plane layer, and select [Create Motion Tween] from the pop-up menu. Frames 1 to 29 will be colored purple in the timeline after the motion tweening is applied.

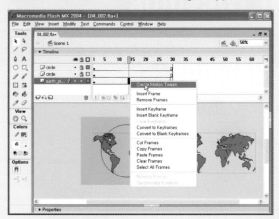

**14** Right-click on the circle layer right above the earth_plane layer and select [Mask] from the pop-up menu.

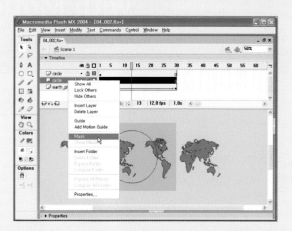

**15** Press [Ctrl]-[Enter] to run the test movie. You should see an animation of a revolving globe.

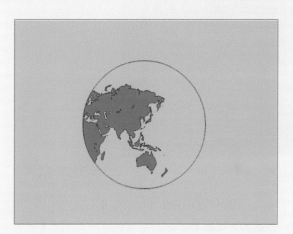

# Simulating Camera Movement with Motion Tweening

In this tutorial, you will motion tween the drawing of a room to simulate camera movement and changes in perspective. To visualize the movie, imagine that you are a movie director looking through the camera's viewfinder. The movie starts with a close-up of a picture hanging above the bed, then the camera moves to the top-left corner of the room and starts backing out the room.

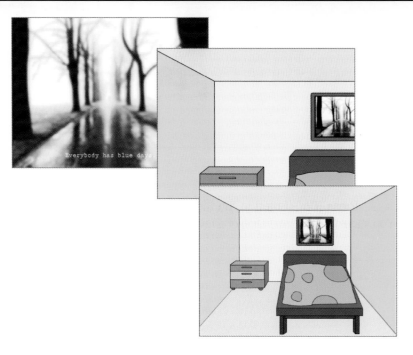

**Start File**
\Sample\Chapter04\04_003.fla

**Final File**
\Sample\Chapter04\04_003_end.fla

## tip >>

### About Motion Tweening

Motion tweening is easy. All you need to do is create the first and last frames of an animation, and Flash fills the in-between frames. To motion tween, the object must either be a symbol or in a group. When used creatively, motion tweening can create a wide range of animation effects, making changes to space, size, color, and transparency.

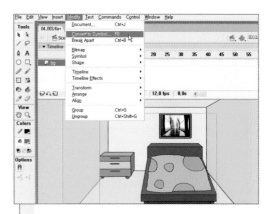

1 Press [Ctrl]-[O] to open the resource file. Press [Ctrl]-[Enter] to run the test movie. You can see that the picture hanging above the bed moves within its frame. This is because it is a movie clip. Next, you need to convert the objects on the stage into symbols in order to apply motion tweening. Click on frame 1 of the bg layer to select all the objects in this frame and select [Modify] - [Convert to Symbol] from the menu bar (or press [F8]).

2 Enter **moving bg** in the name field, set the behavior to Movie Clip, and click [OK].

tip >>

## Setting the Registration Point for a Symbol

The registration point of a symbol is basically the symbol's center of gravity. It's the primary axis point for the symbol as it's being animated.

You can only set the registration point for a symbol in the Convert to Symbol dialog box. By default, the registration point is set in the middle of the symbol. To change its location, click on one of the points on the registration indicator. You can think of a registration point as a pivot. Its location is important when animating a symbol, and your results will vary significantly if you change the registration point location.

When you use actions in your animations, you should note that the default registration point is at the top left coordinate (0,0).

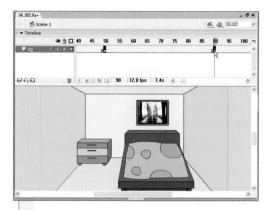

3 Select frame 160 of the bg layer and press [F5] to insert a frame. With the frame rate set to 12 fps, the entire movie will run for 13.3 seconds. Now hold down the [Ctrl] key and select frames 50, 90, and 130. Next, release the [Ctrl] key and press [F6] to insert keyframes which you will use for making changes to the animation.

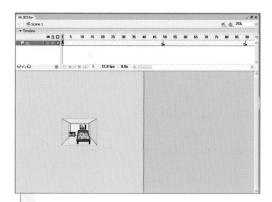

4 As you know, the movie starts with a close-up of the picture hanging above the bed. In the following steps, you'll have to expand the picture to cover the stage completely. First, select frame 1 and reduce the size of the stage to 25%.

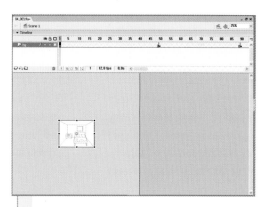

5 As you can see, the room covers the entire stage. Click on the [Show Outline] icon (▢) on the bg layer to show only the room's outline and to reveal the stage. Next, select the Free Transform tool (▦).

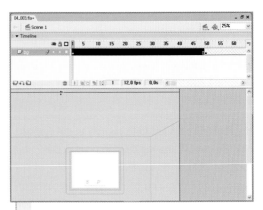

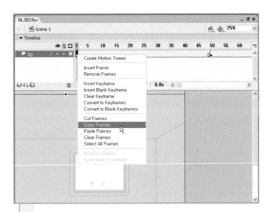

6 Holding down the [Shift] key, click and drag the bounding box handles of the room outwards. As you can see from the figure, the picture has been expanded to fit the stage perfectly.

7 You'll have to make a copy of frame 1 on frame 50 so that the picture is displayed over 50 frames. Right-click on frame 1 and select [Copy Frames] from the pop-up menu.

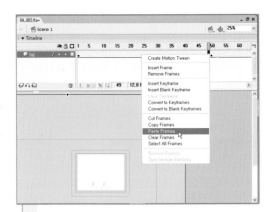

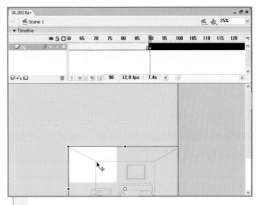

8 Right-click on frame 50 and select [Paste Frames] from the pop-up menu. Another way of making a copy is to select frame 1 and drag it to frame 50 while holding down the [Alt] key. At a frame rate of 12 fps, the picture is shown for about three seconds.

9 In frame 90, the movie will display the upper-left corner of the room. Select frame 90 and use the Free Transform tool (⊞) to expand the room. Position it as shown here.

tip >>

## Tweening Shortcut

In the preceding steps, you had to tween from frames 50 to 90 and then from frames 90 to 130. Since you had keyframes on frames 50, 90, and 130, the instructions were for you to select frames 50 to 130 and then tween everything in one step. But actually, you don't have to select all the frames between frame 50 and frame 130. There's an even faster way.

You only need to make sure that you select the center keyframe (frame 90) and at least one frame each from its left and right. You can select frame 80 to 100, for example, and tween everything from frame 50 to frame 130. You can save a lot of time with this shortcut.

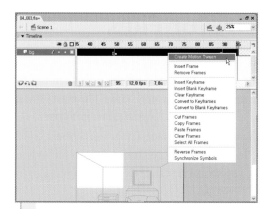

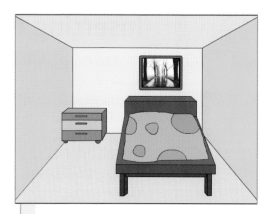

**10** Now that you have created the contents on the keyframes, it's time to animate! Select frames 50 to 130, as shown here, and choose [Create Motion Tween] from the contextual menu.

**11** On the timeline, the motion-tweened frames will be colored light purple. Press [Ctrl]-[Enter] to run Test Movie and check that the animation runs correctly.

**note >>**

Movie clips, like the picture in the tutorial above, run on their own timeline and do not follow the main timeline.

# Inserting Illustrator Files

Adobe Illustrator is a popular vector-based graphics program you can use to draw images that are difficult to draw with Flash alone. Like Illustrator, Flash MX 2004 uses layers. This makes it possible for work done with layers to be shared. Flash files that are exported to Illustrator retain all of their layer properties such as layer name, lock, unlock, hide, show, and so on. When exporting Illustrator files to Flash, you should first save them in versions prior to Illustrator 8.0.

*01* Open Adobe Illustrator and press [Ctrl]-[O] to open the **elly.ai** file from the \Sample\Chapter04\image folder. Click on the [Lock/Unlock] icon (🔒) in the layers palette to lock the layers. Ungroup all objects so that they can be used separately in Flash. When you are done, save the file in a version prior to Illustrator 8.0.

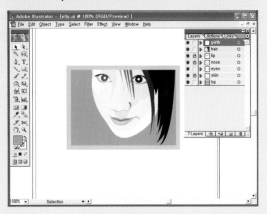

*02* Open Flash. Select [File] - [Import] - [Import to Stage...] from the menu bar. The [Import] command is used to place other types of files into Flash. External files that are imported into Flash are used as objects.

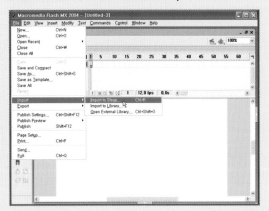

**03** In the Import dialog box, select the **elly.ai** file from the Sample folder and click [Open].

**04** This will open the Illustrator Import dialog box. Under the [Convert] option, check [Layers] and click [OK].

**05** As you can see from the timeline, the layers are imported into Flash with exactly the same properties and stacking order they had in the Illustrator document.

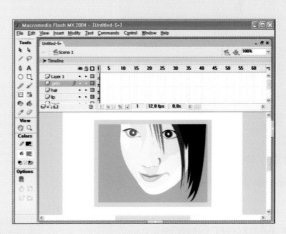

### The Illustrator Import Dialog Box

Ⓐ **Layers**: Converts the layers in the Illustrator document into layers in the Flash document.

Ⓑ **Key Frames**: The layers are imported into Flash as keyframes in the order they were stacked in Illustrator. The layer name becomes the frame label.

Ⓒ **Flatten**: All the layers in the Illustrator document are combined into one layer in the Flash document.

Ⓓ **Include Invisible Layers**: Imports any layers that were hidden in the Illustrator document.

# 3

# Working with Motion Guide Layers

Motion guide layers are used to determine the path of an object during its animation. They are used in more complicated animations where the object doesn't move in a straight line. Lines drawn on the motion guide layer determine the direction of movement for the object. In this example, we will create a motion guide to determine the direction that the boy takes on his snowboard.

**Start File**
\Sample\Chapter04\04_005.fla

**Final File**
\Sample\Chapter04\04_005_end.fla

## Using Motion Guides

Motion guides work best with a single, smooth line without breaks. The object must be aligned with the start and end points of the path in the keyframes at the beginning and end of the animation. When the object is motion tweened, it will follow the line on the motion guide layer.

1 Press [Ctrl]-[O] to open the start file.

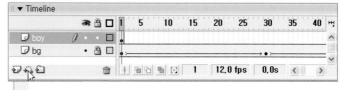

2 Select the boy layer and click on the [Add Motion Guide] icon ( 🔅 ). Then, lock the boy layer by clicking on the [Lock] icon ( 🔒 ).

3 Click on the bg layer and select the Outline option (□). Choose the Pencil tool (✏) and select the Smooth option (⌐S⌐) from the toolbox.

4 Draw a curve on the Guide: boy layer similar to the one shown here. Then lock the Guide: boy layer.

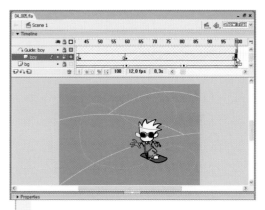

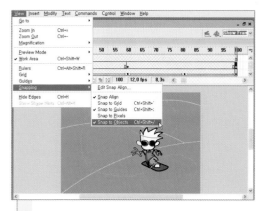

5 Select the boy layer and press [F6] to insert keyframes at frames 30, 43, 60, and 100.

6 Choose [View] - [Snapping] - [Snap to Objects] and make sure that the [Snap to Objects] option is checked.

7 Click on the [Lock] icon (🔒) in the boy layer options while holding down the [Alt] key to unlock the layer.

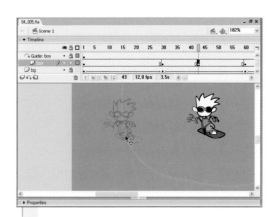

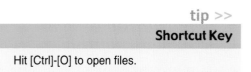

8 The boy symbol must be snapped to the line drawn in the Guide: boy layer to make the motion guide animation work. The symbol contains a small circle with a cross. This is the center point for the symbol. Make sure that the center point is snapped to the starting point of the line.

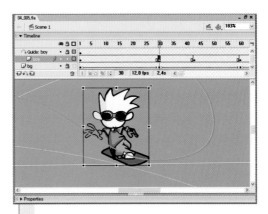

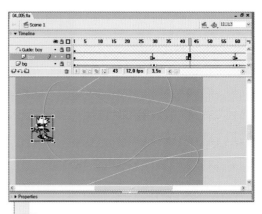

9 Snap the boy symbol in frame 30 to the hill outline and make it slightly larger with the Free Transform tool (⊞).

10 Snap the object in frame 43 to the motion guideline and make it slightly smaller.

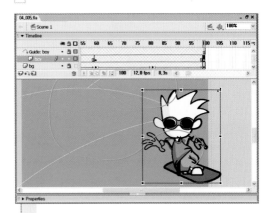

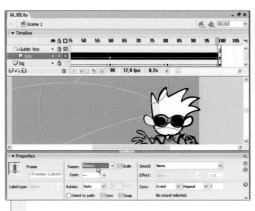

11 At frame 60, snap the object to the motion guide at the right of the stage. Snap the object to the end of the motion guide at frame 100 and make it larger.

12 Select frames 1 through 99 of the boy layer, right-click, and choose [Create Motion Tween].

13 Select a frame between frames 30 and 43 of the boy layer and check the [Orient to Path] option in the Property Inspector.

tip >>
### Orient to Path

This option aligns the baseline of the object to the motion guide.

14. The animation is split into four sections. Select a frame from each section and set the ease values in the Property Inspector as follows: Frames 1-30: **-100**, Frames 30-43: **100**, Frames 43-60: **-100**, Frames 60-100: **100**.

15. Press [Ctrl]-[Enter] to preview the movie.

# Rotating an Object

An object can be rotated during motion tweening; the rotation depends on the center point of the object. The center point of an object can be set while editing the object. In the following examples, you will change the center point of an object to see how this affects the animation.

## Center Point Set in the Center of the Object

**01** Open the start file and press [F6] to insert a keyframe at frame 20.

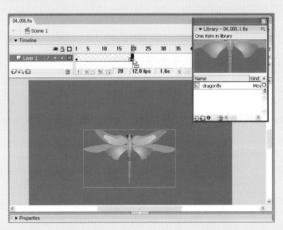

**02** Click frame 1 and, in the Property Inspector, set the tween to Motion and rotate to CW.

*03* Press [Ctrl]-[Enter] to test the movie, then watch how the object rotates.

## Center Point Set Outside of the Object

**Start File**
\Sample\Chapter04\04_006.fla

**Final File**
\Sample\Chapter04\04_006_02_end.fla

*01* Open the start file and double-click the symbol to edit it. In this mode, drag the symbol so that the center point is outside the symbol.

*02* Hit the blue arrow button () to return to the stage and press [F6] to insert a keyframe at frame 20.

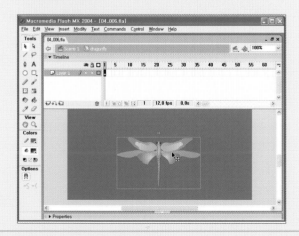

*03* Click frame 1, and in the Property Inspector, set the tween to Motion and rotate to CW.

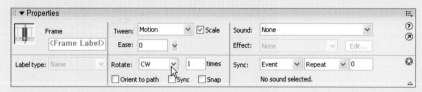

*04* Press [Ctrl]-[Enter] to test the movie. Notice that the object rotates along a different path in this animation.

# Shape Tweening

Shape tweening is used to change the shape of an object. This is also called morphing. Shape tweening is quite different from motion tweening. Shape tweening requires a shape rather than a symbol. It uses symbols that have been broken apart with the Break Apart command or shapes drawn with the drawing tools.

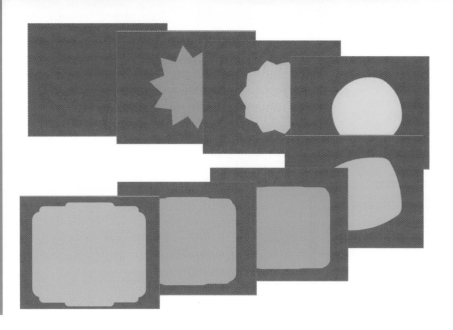

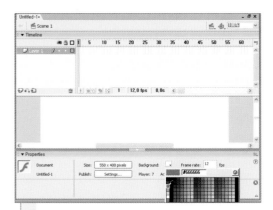

1 Create a new movie using the [Ctrl]-[N] shortcut key and select [Flash Document] from the [General] tab. Set the background color of the new movie to #666666 in the Property Inspector.

2 Choose the PolyStar tool () from the toolbox and click the [Option] button in the Property Inspector to open the Tool Settings dialog box. Set the style to star, the number of sides to 10, and click [OK].

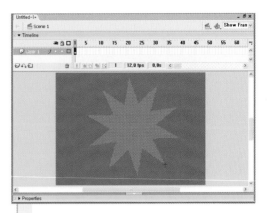

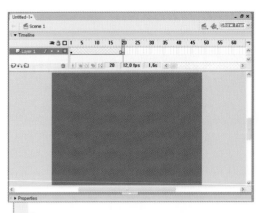

**3** In the toolbox, set the stroke color to no color (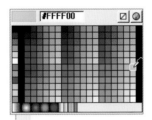) and the fill color to #9900FF. Draw the shape shown here.

**4** Insert a blank keyframe at frame 20 by pressing [F7].

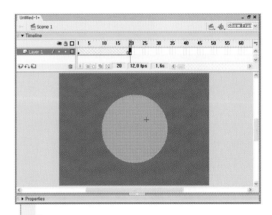

**5** Select the Oval tool and set the stroke color to no color (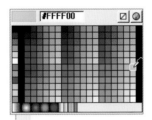) and the fill color to #FFFF00.

**6** Draw a circle on the stage in the same position as the star.

tip >>

### Rectangle Settings

**7** Insert a blank keyframe at frame 40 using the [F7] key. Select the Rectangle tool and click on the Round Rectangle Radius (⌐) option in the toolbox to open the Rectangle Settings dialog box. Set the corner radius to 30 points and click [OK].

If you change the rectangle settings, the settings will apply until they are changed again. In this example, if you draw another rectangle it will have a corner radius of 30 points.

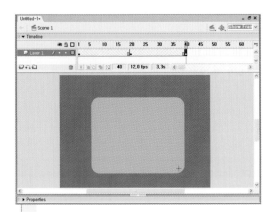

8 Draw the rectangle on the stage as shown here.

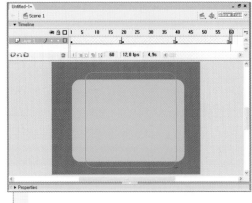

9 Insert a blank keyframe at frame 60 with the [F7] key.

10 Using the Rectangle tool, draw a rounded rectangle and set the fill color to #33CCFF. Draw a second, longer rounded rectangle above it so that the length of this rounded rectangle passes through the rectangle at the bottom. Draw a third long rectangle above the second rectangle. There should be three rounded rectangles that get gradually shorter and wider.

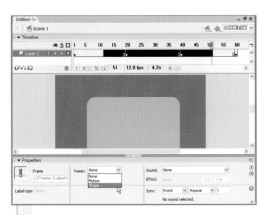

11 Select both the keyframes in frames 20 and 40 and set the tween to Shape in the Property Inspector.

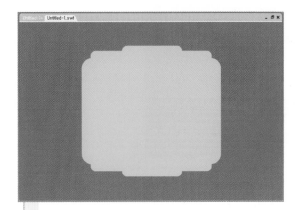

12 Press [Ctrl]-[Enter] to test the movie.

*Exercise*

# 5

# Animating Masks

Masks are used to determine which part of an image will be visible. Masks only affect the layers beneath, and the shape contained on the mask layer indicates what will be visible within the Flash movie. Areas outside of the shape will be hidden. In this exercise, we'll animate the layer mask to create a transition between different bitmap images.

**Final File**

●  \Sample\Chapter04\04_008_end.fla

**Import Files**

●  \Sample\Chapter04\image\snow0.jpg
●  \Sample\Chapter04\image\snow0_1.jpg
●  \Sample\Chapter04\image\snow1.jpg
●  \Sample\Chapter04\image\snow2.jpg
●  \Sample\Chapter04\image\snow3.jpg

1  Use the [Ctrl]-[N] shortcut key to bring up the New Document dialog box and choose the New Document option. Press [Ctrl]-[R] to open the Import dialog box.  Hold down the [Shift] key and select the **snow** files. Click [Open] to import the files.

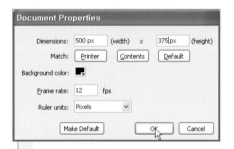

2  Click on the stage and press the [Document Properties] button in the Property Inspector. Set the width to 500 pixels, height to 375 pixels, background color to #000000 (black), and click [OK].

**tip >>**

**[Ctrl]-[R]**

The shortcut key for [File] - [Import] - [Import to Stage] is [Ctrl]-[R].

166

**3** Minimize the timeline and the Property Inspector. Drag a selection box to select all of the images on the stage.

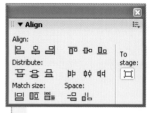

**4** Press [Ctrl]-[K] to open the Align panel. Press the [To Stage] button ([□]) and click the [Align Horizontal Center] ([☐]) and [Align Vertical Center] icons ([☐]) to center the images on the stage. Close the Align panel.

tip >>

## [Align/Distribute to Stage] Button

When you click the [To Stage] button, the options in the Align panel will be applied with respect to the size of the stage. The button will remain pressed until it is clicked again.

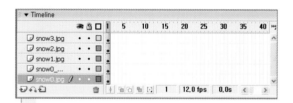

**5** Make sure that all of the images are selected, right-click, and choose [Distribute to Layers].

**6** Show the timeline and drag the layers into the following order: snow0, snow0_1, snow1, snow2, and snow3.

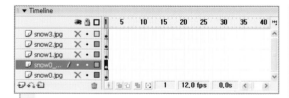

**7** Hold down the [Alt] key and click the Show/Hide option on the snow0_1 layer. All layers except the snow0_1 layer will be hidden.

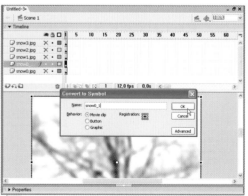

**8** Select the image in the snow0_1 layer and press [F8]. Change the symbol name to **snow0_1** and the behavior to Movie Clip.

9 Insert keyframes at frame 10 and frame 25. Open the Property Inspector and set the alpha value of the instance on frame 25 to 0%.

10 Click between frames 10 to 24, go to the Property Inspector, and set the tween to Motion and ease to -100.

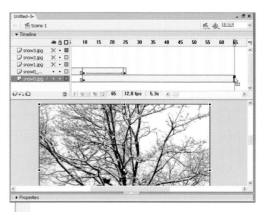

11 Hold down the [Alt] key and click the Show/Hide option of the snow0_1 layer to show all the layers. Click the snow0 layer and drag frame 1 to frame 10.

12 Click frame 65 and press [F5] to insert frames 10 to 65 on the snow0 layer.

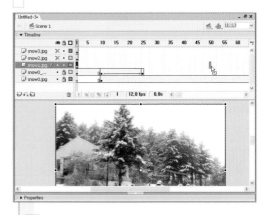

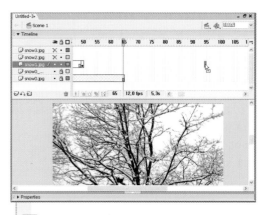

13 Move frame 1 of the snow1 layer to frame 50.

14 Select frame 95 of the snow1 layer and press [F5] to insert frames.

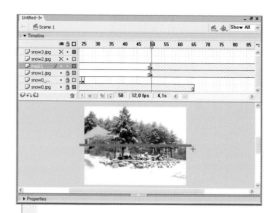

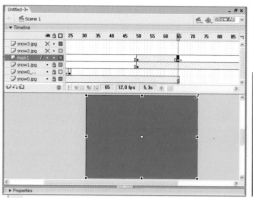

**15** Select the snow1 layer and click on the [Insert Layer] icon ( ) to insert a new layer. Name the layer **mask1**. Select frame 50 of the mask1 layer and press [F6] to insert a keyframe.

**16** Using the Rectangle tool, draw in a rectangle as shown above. Use the [F8] shortcut key to register the rectangle as a movie clip symbol.

**17** Select frame 65 of the mask1 layer and press [F6] to insert a keyframe. Use the Free Transform tool to increase the size of the rectangle so that it is slightly larger than the stage.

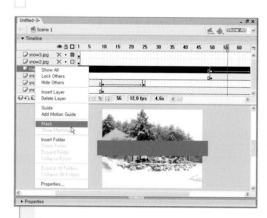

**18** Insert a motion tween between frames 50 and 65. At frame 66, press [F7] to insert a blank keyframe.

**19** Right-click the mask1 layer and select [Mask].

note >>

Objects on a mask layer are used to determine what will show on the layers underneath-so when you draw on a mask layer, you can select any color. However, you must make sure that the shape has no lines as these will be ignored in a layer mask.

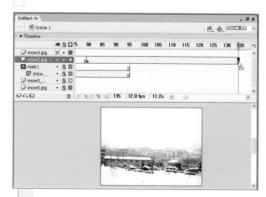

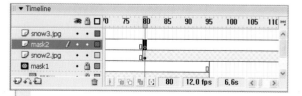

**20** Select the snow2 layer and drag frame 1 to frame 80. Click frame 135 and press [F5] to insert frames.

**21** Select the snow2 layer and click on the [Insert Layer] icon ( ) to add a layer. Name it **mask2**. At frame 80, press [F6] to insert a keyframe.

169

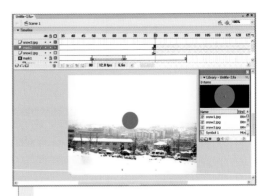

**22** Use the Oval tool to draw a circle and register it as a movie clip symbol.

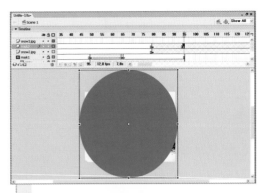

**23** Insert a keyframe at frame 95 and use the Free Transform tool to increase the size of the symbol so that it is slightly larger than the stage.

tip >>

## To Preview Mask Effects

When a mask is created, the mask and layers beneath that are masked will be locked. You can only preview a mask effect on the stage when these layers are locked. Locking the layers has no effect on the published movie.

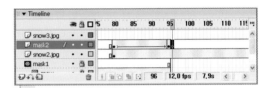

**24** Insert a motion tween between frames 80 and 95.  At frame 96, press [F7] to insert a blank keyframe. Right-click on the mask2 layer and select [Mask].

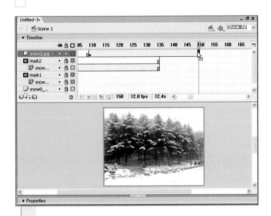

**25** Move frame 1 of the snow3 layer to frame 110.

**26** Select frame 150 and press [F5] to insert frames.

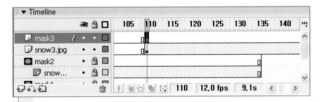

**27** Select the snow3 layer, click the [Insert Layer] icon () to insert a layer, and name it **mask3**. At frame 110, press [F6] to insert a keyframe.

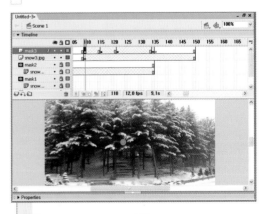

**28** Use the Oval tool ( ⬭ ) to draw a small circle as shown above.

170

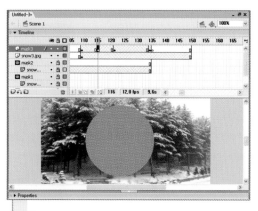

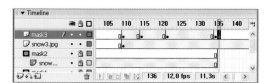

29 Insert keyframes at frames 115, 122, and 135. At frame 136, use [F7] to insert a blank keyframe.

30 Make the circle in frame 115 smaller in size.

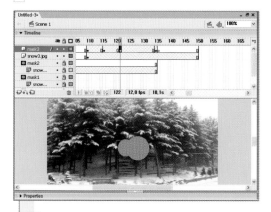

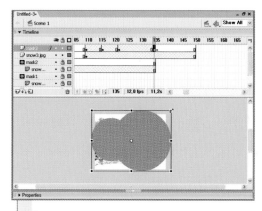

31 At frame 122, draw a larger circle next to the smaller circle. The two circles should be touching as shown above.

32 Select frame 122, hold down the [Alt] key and drag it to frame 135 to create a copy. Use the Free Transform tool ( ⊞ ) to make the two circles larger than the stage, as shown above.

**tip >>**

If you hold down the [Alt] key as you increase the size of an object, the size will increase evenly from the object's center.

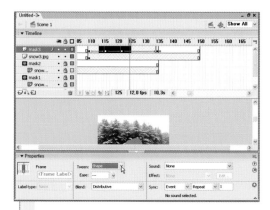

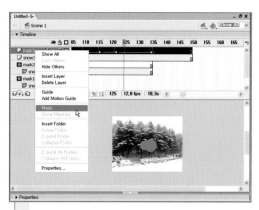

33 Select the frames from 110 to 135 and select Shape Tween in the Property Inspector.

34 Right-click the mask3 layer and select [Mask].

## Creating Mask Animation

When you create an animation using a mask, there are two things to consider so that the animation works properly.

First, if there are two or more groups or instances in the mask layer, the animation may recognize only one group or instance–or none at all.

Second, if you want to use text as a mask, you must break apart the text. The shortcut to do this is [Ctrl]-[B].

35 Press [Ctrl]-[Enter] to preview your work.

# 6

# E-Card Animation Using a Motion Guide Mask

In the last exercise of this chapter, you will learn to use a combination of techniques to create an e-card. You will use motion tweening to move the background elements and a motion guide layer to simulate the erratic movements of a butterfly. In addition, you will use a layer mask on a text layer so that the end result is a greeting that scrolls in the middle of the card.

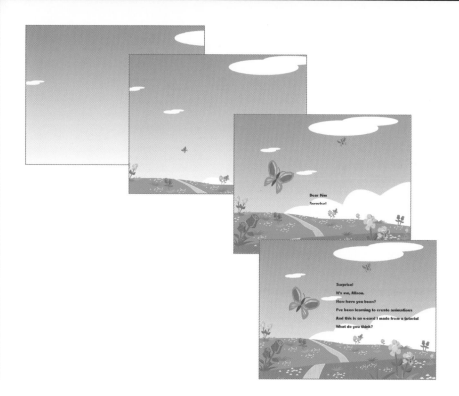

**Start File**
- \Sample\Chapter04\04_009.fla

**Final File**
- \Sample\Chapter04\04_009_end.fla

## tip >>

### Inserting Frames

When you look at the timeline it appears that it only contains up to 750 frames. However, if you add frames, the timeline length will increase. Click frame 700 and press [F5] to insert frames. You will then be able to click on frame 1,000 and add more frames with the [F5] key.

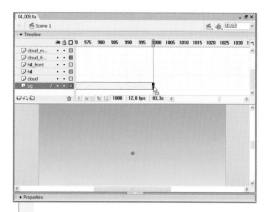

[1] Open the start file and insert 1,000 frames on the bg layer. You can do this by clicking the last frame and pressing the [F5] key.

2 Select the cloud layer and insert keyframes into frames 75 and 213 with the [F6] key. Increase the total number of frames to 1,000.

3 Select frame 213 and move the back_cloud symbol from below the stage so that the top of the symbol reaches the middle of the stage.

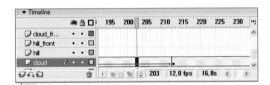

4 Right-click between frames 75 and 212 of the cloud layer and select [Create Motion Tween] from the shortcut menu.

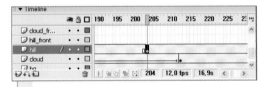

5 Add keyframes to the hill layer at frames 61 and 204. Increase the total number of frames to 1,000.

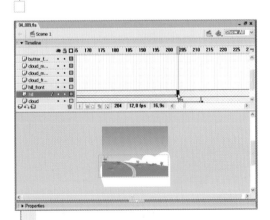

6 Select frame 204 and move the objects on the hill layer slightly below the back_cloud symbol on the cloud layer.

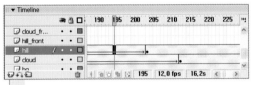

7 Right-click between frames 61 and 203 of the hill layer and add a motion tween.

8 Select the hill_front layer and insert keyframes at frames 96 and 240. Increase the total frames to 1,000.

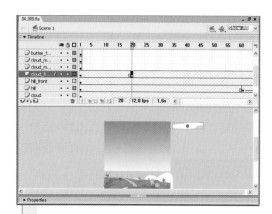

**9** Select frame 240 of the hill_front layer and position the objects slightly below the hill layer objects.

**10** Right-click between frames 96 and 239 and add a motion tween. Select the cloud_front layer and insert a keyframe at frame 20. Insert frames until you have a total of 1,000.

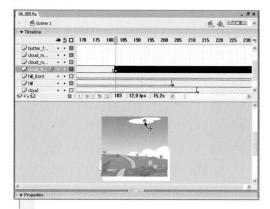

**11** Insert a keyframe into frame 183 and move the cloud symbol onto the stage.

**12** Right-click between frames 22 and 182 and add a motion tween.

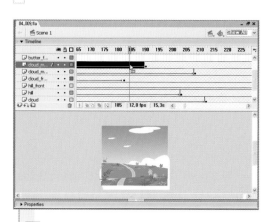

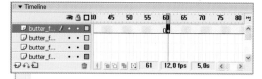

**14** We want the fly symbol in the butter_fly 4 layer to move with the hill layer. First, make frame 1,000 the last frame and insert a keyframe in frame 61.

**13** Using the same approach, add a motion tween to the cloud_middle layer between frames 1 and 209 so that the cloud moves onto the stage. On the cloud_middle 2 layer, motion tween frames 6 through 292 to move the cloud onto the stage. Increase the number of frames on both layers to a total of 1,000.

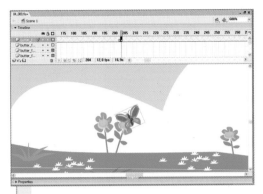

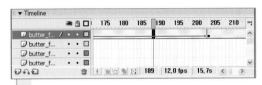

15 Insert a keyframe in frame 204 and adjust the fly symbol so that it is always on top of the first flower.

16 Motion tween the area between frames 61 and 203.

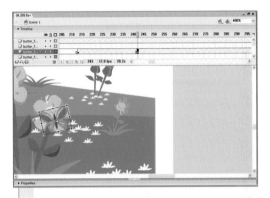

17 Selecting the butter_fly 2 layer, move frame 1 to frame 214. Make frame 1,000 the last frame.

18 Select and insert a keyframe into frame 243. Arrange the fly symbol so that it is on top of the flower and make it slightly smaller.

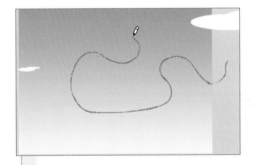

19 Motion tween the area between frames 214 and 242.

20 Select the butter_fly 3 layer, and click the [Add Motion Guide] icon (⊕). This creates a new layer that will be used to guide the motion of the butterfly symbol.

21 Press [F7] at frame 55 to insert a blank keyframe. Use the Pencil tool to draw the line shown above. This will become the flight path for the butterfly.

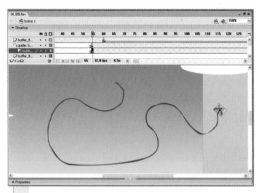

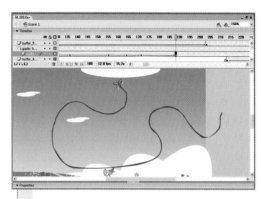

22 Press the [F6] key at frame 55 of the butter_fly 3 layer to insert a keyframe, then drag the butterfly symbol to the start of the motion guide.

23 Add another keyframe at frame 189 and drag the butterfly to the end of the motion guide. If you drag the playhead, you will see the butterfly following the path in the motion guide layer.

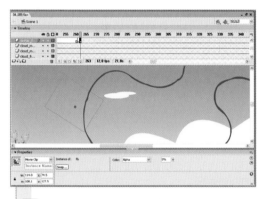

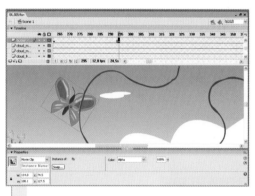

24 Use the Selection tool to drag frame 1 of the butter_fly 1 layer to frame 263. In the color mixer, set the alpha value of the fly symbol to 0%.

25 Insert a keyframe at frame 295 and set the alpha value to 100%.

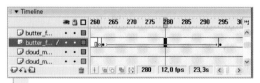

26 Create a motion tween between frames 263 and 295.

27 Select the butter_fly 4 layer and click the [Insert Layer] icon (⬛) to add a layer. Name the new layer **text**.

28 Choose the Text tool and make the following changes in the Property Inspector. Font: **Arial Black**, Font Size: **20**, and Font Color: **#660000**.

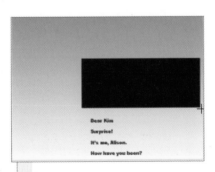

29 Type the text shown here onto the stage. You can change the names, write it in your own words, and send this card to a friend. The width and length of the text should approximate what is shown here.

30 Select the text layer, add another layer, and call it **text_mask**.

31 Use the Rectangle tool to draw a rectangle above the text as shown above.

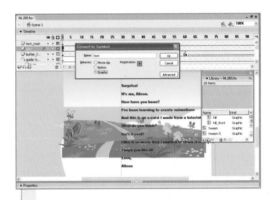

32 Select the rectangle and press [F8] to convert the object into a symbol. Set the name to **text** and the behavior to Movie Clip.

**33** Drag frame 1 of the text layer to frame 269. Add a keyframe to frame 656 and move the text to the top, above the rectangle on the text_mask layer.

**34** Motion tween frames 269 to 656. Press [F7] at frame 657 to insert a blank keyframe.

**35** Right-click on the text_mask layer and select [Mask] from the shortcut menu.

**36** Press [Ctrl]-[Enter] to preview the final movie.

## A Final Note

When creating a Flash movie, it's very easy to get carried away and add too many animation effects, so it's important that you understand the need to use animations appropriately. Sometimes less is more! In addition, the more elaborate your animation, the larger the file size is likely to be.

Flash can add excitement to static Web sites, but it's important to balance the impact of your movie against the extra time it will take to load the Web site. Most visitors come to a Web site in search of information. An animation that prevents them from accessing the information quickly will be a source of frustration, particularly if the animation takes time to load.

Many Web sites include a large introductory animation that can take time to load. From the visitor's point of view, this could be seen as unnecessary. If you decide to include a Flash introduction, add a [Skip Intro] button to address this concern.

Flash should be used to enhance the Web site experience. Use it to create tools that help users and simplify the Web interface. Large movies meant to display your skills as an animator are not always appropriate!

**Chapter** 5

# A Must for Designers - Using Behaviors to Learn ActionScript

In the last chapter, you learned to create animations using frame-by-frame animation, shape tweening, and motion tweening. These are linear animations that are placed on the timeline and played in order. In this chapter, you will learn to create non-linear animations using ActionScript. A non-linear animation does not always play in the order shown in the timeline. Using ActionScript, a user can control the order that an animation is played to create an interactive experience for viewers.

# Actions and Behaviors

ActionScript is Flash's own programming language, and advanced Flash designers use it to create very complicated movies. In this chapter, you will learn to insert some basic and common actions using the Behaviors and Actions panels. This lets you add interactivity to your movies without having to learn or write that much code.

## Understanding the Behaviors Panel

The Behaviors panel is used to add interactivity to movies within Flash, and provides an easy way to create ActionScript. Instead of entering the ActionScript into the Actions panel, selecting a behavior will generate the script for you. You can bring up the Behaviors panel with [Shift]-[F3] or by selecting [Window] - [Development Panels] - [Behaviors].

The Behaviors panel contains actions to make it easy to work with movie clips, sound, and video. Select the object that the behavior is to be applied to and select the behavior to apply.

New behaviors can be downloaded from the Macromedia Exchange site (www.macromedia.com/exchange).

## About Movie Clip Behaviors

The Behaviors panel contains twelve behaviors that relate specifically to movie clips. The details of each of these behaviors are listed on the following page.

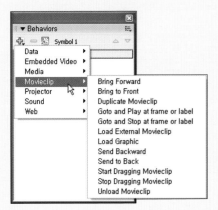

## Behaviors to Control Movie Clips

| Behavior | Purpose | Information Required |
|---|---|---|
| Bring Forward | Brings the target movie clip one position higher in the stacking order. | Instance name of movie clip. |
| Bring to Front | Brings the target movie clip to the top of the stacking order; the clip appears on top of all other clips on the stage. | Instance name of movie clip. |
| Duplicate a Movieclip | Duplicates movie clip. | • Instance name of movie clip to duplicate.<br>• X-offset and Y-offset: Position of duplicate from original in pixels. |
| Goto and Play at frame or label | Plays a movie clip from a specified frame. | • Instance name of movie clip to play.<br>• Frame number or label to play from. |
| Goto and Stop at frame or label | Stops a movie clip, optionally moving the playhead to a specified frame. | • Instance name of target clip to stop.<br>• Frame number or label to stop at. |
| Load External Movieclip | Loads an external SWF file into a target movie clip. | • URL/filename of external SWF file.<br>• Instance name of movie clip or screen in which to load the SWF file. |
| Load Graphic | Loads an external JPEG file into a movie clip. | • Path and filename of JPEG file.<br>• Instance name of movie clip in which to load the graphic. |
| Send Backward | Sends the target movie clip one position lower in the stacking order. | Instance name of movie clip. |
| Send to Back | Sends the target movie clip to the bottom of the stacking order; the clip appears underneath all other clips on the stage. | Instance name of movie clip. |
| Start Dragging Movieclip | Starts dragging a movie clip. | Instance name of movie clip. |
| Stop Dragging Movieclip | Stops the dragging action. | – |
| Unload Movieclip | Removes an SWF file loaded with the Load Movie behavior or action. | Instance name of movie clip to unload. |

## Using Behaviors to Load Images

Flash allows you to load an image while a movie is playing using the [Movieclip] - [Load Graphic] behavior. This is normally used to load an image when a button is clicked. The image is then loaded into an existing movie clip that is already positioned on the stage.

### The Load Graphic Dialog Box

Ⓐ Enter the URL or filename of the image to be loaded.

Ⓑ Select the movie clip instance into which the graphic is to be loaded.

Ⓒ Click here to enter the movie clip based on its relative path.

Ⓓ Click here to enter the movie clip based on its absolute path.

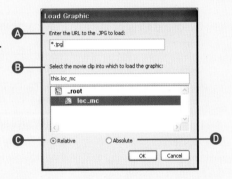

### Relative and Absolute Paths

Whenever you refer to an instance name, you can use either a relative or absolute path. Relative paths create references to the instance from the current position within the movie, whereas absolute paths give the complete reference from the main timeline. Relative paths can only be used for movie clips that are below the current movie clip. Within this example, we will use relative paths to specify the video clip instance that we want to target.

## Using Behaviors to Control Video Clips

Creating ActionScript that controls video clips can be complicated. It is often easier to use the Embedded Video commands in the Behaviors panel. You can use these behaviors to generate actions that play, pause, stop, show, hide, fast forward, and rewind a video clip.

**Behaviors to Control Video Clips**

| Behavior | Explanation | Parameters |
|----------|-------------|------------|
| Play Video | Plays a video clip. | Instance name of the video clip to play. |
| Stop Video | Stops the video. | Instance name of the video clip to stop. |
| Pause Video | Pauses the video. | Instance name of the video clip to pause. |
| Rewind Video | Rewinds the video by the number of frames specified. | • Instance name of the video clip to rewind. <br> • Number of frames to rewind. |
| Fast Forward Video | Fast-forwards the video by the number of frames specified. | • Instance name of the video clip to fast forward. <br> • Number of frames. |
| Hide Video | Hides the video clip. | Instance name of the video clip to hide from view. |
| Show Video | Shows the video. | Instance name of the video clip to show. |

## Understanding the Actions Panel

ActionScript is made up of a series of actions written within the Actions panel, and it is important to become familiar with this area of Flash. You can open the Actions panel by pressing the [F9] key or by selecting [Window] - [Development Panels] - [Actions]. The actions for the selected frame, button, or movie instance will be displayed.

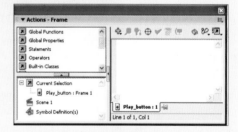

## Placing ActionScript within a Movie

There are three places in a movie where you can add ActionScript–a frame, button, or movie. Which option you go with depends on the effect that you are trying to achieve. Your actions can be entered into these areas using the Actions panel.

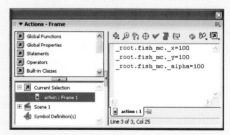

Adding Actions to a Frame

Actions added to a frame are often used to determine how a movie will play. You can only add actions to a keyframe. To do this, click the keyframe and press [F9] to display the Actions - Frame panel.

Actions associated with buttons are usually added to control what happens when the button is clicked. You can add ActionScript by selecting the button instance on the stage and pressing the [F9] key to show the Actions - Button panel.

Movie instances often use ActionScript to make something happen when the mouse pointer moves. Select the movie clip instance on the stage and press the [F9] key to access the Actions - Movie Clip panel.

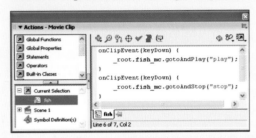

# The Key Areas of the Actions Panel

The Actions panel is made up of several areas.

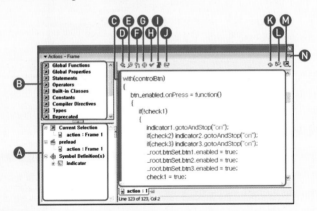

### Ⓐ Script Navigator

The script navigator contains information about a symbol, instance, or scene name. You can use it to display scripts that relate to the selected item.

### Ⓑ Actions Toolbox

The toolbox contains all actions organized into categories that are displayed in a tree structure. You can either double-click an action or drag it to the script window.

186

### ⊙ Script Window

The script window contains the actions that make up your ActionScript. Actions are added by selecting them from the actions toolbox or by typing in the relevant commands.

### ⊙ Add a New Item to the Script

You can also use the [Add] menu to add actions to the script pane. Click the + sign and navigate to the appropriate action.

### ⊙ Find

Find can be used to search for specific words in the Actions panel.

### ⊙ Replace

Replace can be used to replace a word in the Actions panel with another word.

### ⊙ Insert a Target Path

Insert a Target Path shows a tree structure listing the path to all instances on the stage. A path is a way to add actions to an object.

### ⊙ Check Syntax

Check Syntax is used to check that you have entered ActionScript correctly.

### ⊙ Auto Format

Auto Format aligns the ActionScript or fills in missing statements.

### ⊙ Show Code Hint

Show Code Hint is used to display information for the current ActionScript command. A keyword list may appear showing a selection of options to choose from. You may also see a pop-up tool tip telling you what information is needed.

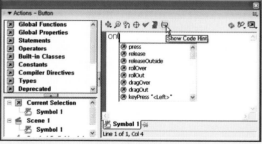

### ⊙ Reference

Reference displays the Help panel.

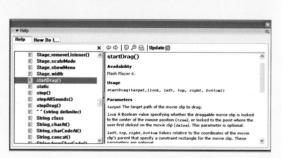

## ⓛ Debug Options

Debug Options is used to locate and correct errors in ActionScript. Debugging is commonly used by programmers.

## ⓜ View Options

View Options shows the display options for the script window. The following options are included.

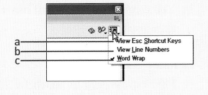

**a. View Esc Shortcut Keys:** When this option is selected, the toolbox and the [Add a New Item to the Script] menus () show the [Esc] shortcut keys for each action.

**b. View Line Numbers:** Displays the line number at the left of the script window.

**c. Word Wrap:** When Word Wrap is selected, scripts longer than one line will automatically wrap to the next line.

## ⓝ Options Menu

The Options menu shows options for the Actions panel including Go to Line, Find, Replace, Import, and Export Script.

## Controlling a Movie with Actions

Actions can be used to control the way a movie plays. The most commonly used actions are those that control frames such as play(), stop(), gotoAndStop(), and gotoAndPlay(). These commands allow frames to be played in any order instead of relying on the timeline to play them one at a time.

### Actions for Controlling Frames

| Action | Effect |
|--------|--------|
| play() | Play the movie from the current frame. |
| stop() | Stop the movie at the current frame. |
| gotoAndPlay() | Move to the specified frame and play the movie.<br><br>• gotoAndPlay(10) - Move to frame 10 and play the movie.<br>• gotoAndPlay("start") - Move to the frame labeled "start" and play the movie. |
| gotoAndStop() | Move to the specified frame and stop playing the movie.<br><br>• gotoAndStop(10) - Move to frame 10 and stop playing the movie.<br>• gotoAndStop("start") - Move to the frame labeled "start" and stop playing the movie. |

## Setting Movie Clip Properties with Actions

Characteristics of a movie clip, such as its size, height, and position on the stage, can be controlled using ActionScript. These characteristics are referred to as the properties of the movie clip. All properties in ActionScript have a name that starts with the underscore character (_). You can change a movie clip's properties by referring to its instance name.

There are two types of movie clip properties: those that you can view or get properties for (i.e., read-only) and those that you can both read and set.

All movie clip instances on the stage have x, y coordinates; width; height; object size; and xscale/yscale properties. ActionScript can read and set these properties as part of an animation.

The following table shows a list of the commonly used properties and their characteristics.

## Properties and Characteristics of Movie Clips

| Property | Get | Set | Explanation |
|---|---|---|---|
| _x | yes | yes | Indicates the x coordinate of the movie clip instance on the stage (from left to right from the left edge of the stage). |
| | | | ball._x = 200;<br>This code sets the position of the ball movie clip instance to 200 pixels from the left of the stage.<br><br>ball._x += 4;<br>The line above increases the x coordinate of the ball movie clip by 4 pixels. |
| _y | yes | yes | Indicates the y coordinate of the instance on the stage (from up to down from the top edge of the stage.) |
| | | | ball._y = 200;<br>The line above sets the position of the ball movie clip instance to 200 pixels from the top of the stage.<br><br>ball._y += 4;<br>This example increases the x coordinate of the ball movie clip by 4 pixels. |
| _width | yes | yes | Indicates the width of the movie clip instance. |
| | | | ball._width = 100;<br>This example sets the width of the ball movie clip instance to 100 pixels.<br><br>ball._width -=10;<br>The line above reduces the width of the ball movie clip instance by 10 pixels. |
| _height | yes | yes | Indicates the height of the movie clip instance. |
| | | | ball._height = 100;<br>This example sets the height of the ball movie clip instance to 100 pixels.<br><br>ball._height -=10;<br>The line above reduces the height of the ball movie clip instance by 10 pixels. |
| _alpha | yes | yes | Indicates the transparency of the movie clip instance. |
| | | | The alpha property can be a value from 0% to 100%. A value of 0% is invisible while a value of 100% is opaque.<br><br>ball._alpha -= 10;<br>This example reduces the alpha value of the ball movie clip instance by 10%. |
| _rotation | yes | yes | Indicates the clockwise rotation of the instance in degrees. |
| | | | ball._rotation += 5;<br>The line above rotates the ball movie clip instance by 5 degrees clockwise. |
| _visible | yes | yes | Indicates the visibility of the instance–either true or false. |
| | | | ball._visible =false;<br>Setting the _visible property to false hides the ball movie clip instance.<br>**Note**: The instance will be visible on the stage and will only be hidden when the movie is tested. |

**Other Movie Clip Properties**

| Property | Explanation |
|----------|-------------|
| _currentframe | Shows the number of the current frame in the movie clip. |
| _frameloaded | Shows how many frames in the movie clip have been loaded. |
| _name | Refers to the instance name of the movie clip. |
| _target | Specifies the movie clip target. |
| _totalframes | Shows the total number of frames in the movie clip. |
| _url | Shows the URL of the SWF file from which the movie clip was loaded. |
| _xmouse | Shows the x coordinate of the mouse cursor. |
| _xscale | Specifies the size using the horizontal scale of the movie. |
| _ymouse | Shows the y coordinate of the mouse cursor. |
| _yscale | Specifies the size using the vertical scale of the movie. |

# Dragging a Movie Clip

The startDrag() and stopDrag() actions allow you to drag a movie clip around the stage using your mouse. These actions allow the user to interact with the Flash movie and are useful in games and creating customized mouse cursors. The startDrag() and stopDrag() actions can also be used to create moveable menu panels like the Actions panel.

Once a startDrag() action is applied to a movie clip instance you will be able to drag it around the stage until you apply a startDrag() action to a different instance or until you apply the stopDrag() action. The stopDrag() action doesn't require the name of a movie clip instance. You can only drag one movie clip at a time.

**startDrag() and stopDrag() Actions**

| Action | Explanation |
|--------|-------------|
| startDrag() | Allows a movie clip instance to be dragged by the mouse; requires the instance name of the movie clip.<br><br>**startDrag("fish");**<br><br>The startDrag() action is applied to the fish movie clip instance on the stage.<br><br>**startDrag("fish", true);**<br><br>A value of 'true' means that that the center of the movie clip is locked to the center of the mouse pointer.<br><br>**StartDrag("fish",true, 50,50,200,200);**<br><br>Specifying rectangular coordinates keeps the movement of the movie clip within that area. If you don't specify coordinates, the movie clip can be moved anywhere on the stage. |
| stopDrag() | Ends the drag action that was started with the last startDrag() action. |

# The fscommand Action

While you normally work with (FLA) files in Flash, it can also generate Shockwave Flash files (SWF) and Flash Projector files (EXE or HQX) for use on the Internet or CD-ROMs. Flash Projector files are basically SWF files that come with the Flash Player. The fscommand can be used to set display options for SWF and Projector files. The fscommand can also be used to send information to the Web browser that opens the SWF movie.

You can use the Flash Player fscommand either with Projector files or with SWF files that are opened in the Flash Player. In these cases, the fscommand can be used to maximize the window of the Flash Player file, allow scaling of the movie, show or hide the menu, determine whether the file responds to keystrokes, run an external program, or close the Flash Player.

The fscommand has six commands. Each of these commands has a parameter. Each time you use the fscommand you will normally need to supply two pieces of information or arguments.

## Fscommand Actions

| Action | Explanation |
|--------|-------------|
| fscommand | **fscommand("command" , "parameters");**<br>Command: The name of the command being sent.<br>Parameters: Parameters sent with the command. |
| | **fscommand("fullscreen", true);**<br>The fullscreen command determines how the Flash Player window will be sized. Setting the parameter to true displays the Flash movie in full-screen mode. |
| | **fscommand("allowscale", false);**<br>The allowscale command is used to specify if the Flash movie is to be shown at the stage size or if it is to be scaled to fit the size of the Flash Player window. A setting of true scales the movie while false keeps the movie at the original size. |
| | **fscommand("showmenu", false);**<br>Showmenu determines whether or not to display the full standalone Flash menu when the movie is right-clicked. The false parameter means that only the [About Flash Player] item will be displayed and other items will be dimmed. |
| | **fscommand("quit");**<br>The quit command does not have any parameters and is used to quit the Flash Player. |
| | **fscommand("exec","NOTEPAD.exe");**<br>The exec command is used to open an external program. |
| | **fscommand("trapallkeys", false)**<br>The trapallkeys command determines whether letters typed on the keyboard are sent through to the Flash Player. Setting the parameter to false prevents the user from being able to interact with the movie using the keyboard. |

## Button Event Handlers

Event handlers allow Flash to respond to events such as clicking a mouse or moving a mouse over an object. An event handler determines what happens when the event takes place. For example, the onRelease event could be used to say that when a button is clicked, a specific frame in the movie is played.

Actions are applied to button instances using the following format.

| Format | on (Event){<br>   //action script<br>   } |
|---|---|

note >>

Lines starting with // are comments and won't be processed by Flash. You can use them to write yourself notes about the ActionScript without affecting the movie.

There are eight different button event handlers that you can use to control your movie.

### Button Event Handlers

| Event | Event Happens When: |
|---|---|
| press | The button is pressed while the pointer is over the button's hit area. |
| release | The button is released while the pointer is over the button's hit area. |
| releaseOutside | The button is released while the pointer is outside the button's hit area. |
| rollOver | The pointer is moved over the button's hit area. |
| rollOut | The pointer is moved from the button's hit area to outside of the button's hit area. |
| dragOver | The pointer is moved over the button's hit area while the mouse button is held down. |
| dragOut | The pointer is moved from the button's hit area to outside of the hit area while the mouse button is held down. |
| keyPress "< >" | A specified key on the keyboard is pressed. |

# Adding Actions to Frames and Buttons

This example uses button event handlers and movie control actions to play and stop the animation. In this animation, the cartoon character flies across the screen or stops in the middle depending on whether you click the start or stop button.

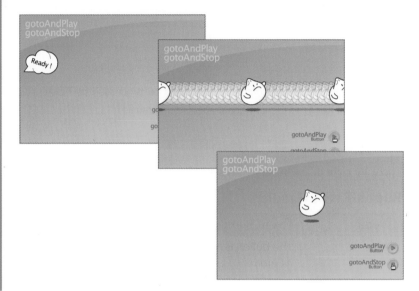

**Start File**
\Sample\Chapter05\05_001.fla

**Final File**
\Sample\Chapter05\05_001_end.fla

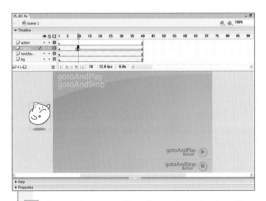

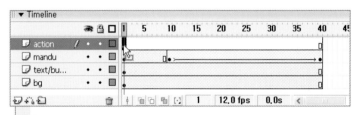

1 Open the start file. Drag the playhead to see the animation of the cartoon character from frame 10 to frame 40. Select the [View Line Numbers] option from [View Options].

2 Select frame 1 of the action layer and press [F9] to open the Actions panel.

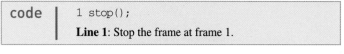

```
code    1 stop();
        Line 1: Stop the frame at frame 1.
```

**note >>**

ActionScript lines that don't end with a { or } should end with a semicolon.

**3** To stop the animation from playing, type **stop();** into the script window. This adds the stop() action to the keyframe at frame 1. Press [Ctrl]-[Enter] to test that the animation stops in frame 1.

```
code    1 on(release){
        2  gotoAndPlay(10);
        3 }
```

**Lines 1~3**: This code reacts to the on(Release) event handler (i.e., it occurs when the button is clicked).
**Line 2**: Move to frame 10 and play the movie.

**4** Return to the movie and select the gotoAndPlay button instance on the bottom-right corner of the stage. Enter the ActionScript below in the Actions panel.

```
code    1 on(release){
        2  gotoAndStop(25);
        3 }
```

**Lines 1~3**: This code reacts to the on(Release) event handler (i.e., it occurs when the button is clicked).
**Line 2**: Move to frame 25 and stop playing the movie.

**5** Select the gotoAndStop button at the bottom-right corner of the screen and enter the following ActionScript in the Actions panel.

6 Test the movie with [Ctrl]-[Enter]. When the gotoAndPlay button is clicked, the character will move from left to right across the stage. When the gotoAndStop button is selected, the character will stop in the middle of the screen.

# 2

# Controlling Movie Clip Properties

In this example, we will learn how to change the properties such as _xscale, _yscale, _rotation, _x, _y, and _alpha using ActionScript. We will create a movie in which buttons are used to set the properties of a movie clip instance.

**Start File**
└─ ● \Sample\Chapter05\05_002.fla

**Final File**
└─ ● \Sample\Chapter05\05_002_end.fla

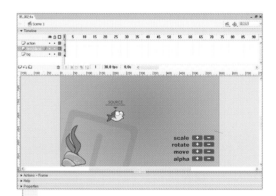

1 Open the start file. It contains a fish movie clip instance in an underwater setting. It also contains buttons titled scale, rotation, move, and alpha.

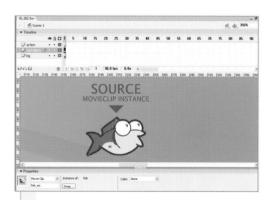

2 Select the fish movie clip from the stage and enter the instance name **fish_mc** in the Property Inspector.

tip >>

## Naming Instances

Get into the habit of naming each instance on the stage. This is crucial when working with ActionScript. You can give names to buttons, movie clips, and some types of text fields. Naming these objects tells ActionScript which object you want to affect, so it is important that each name is unique.

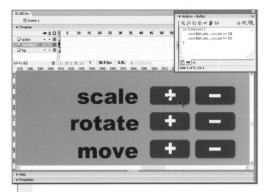

3 Select the Increase Scale button on the stage and press [F9] to open the Actions panel.

**code**

```
1 on(release){
2 _root.fish_mc._xscale += 10;
3 _root.fish_mc._yscale += 10;
4 }
```

**Lines 1~4**: Actions will be triggered by the on(Release) event (i.e., a mouse click).

**Line 2**: Increases (+=) the xscale property of the fish_mc movie clip instance by 10%.

**Line 3**: Increases (+=) the yscale property of the fish_mc movie clip instance by 10%.

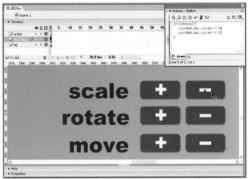

4 Enter the following actions for the Decrease button.

**code**

```
1 on(release){
2 _root.fish_mc._xscale -= 10;
3 _root.fish_mc._yscale -= 10;
4 }
```

**Lines 1~4**: Actions will be triggered by the on(Release) event (i.e., a mouse click).

**Line 2**: Decreases (-=) the x-scale property of the fish_mc movie clip instance by 10%.

**Line 3**: Decreases (-=) the y-scale property of the fish_mc movie clip instance by 10%.

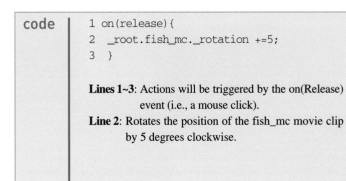

**code**

```
1 on(release){
2 _root.fish_mc._rotation +=5;
3 }
```

**Lines 1~3**: Actions will be triggered by the on(Release) event (i.e., a mouse click).

**Line 2**: Rotates the position of the fish_mc movie clip by 5 degrees clockwise.

5 The Rotate Increase button contains the following actions.

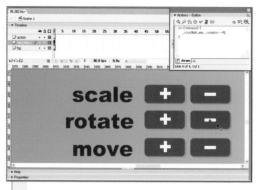

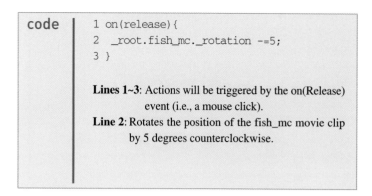

```
code    1 on(release){
        2 _root.fish_mc._rotation -=5;
        3 }
```

**Lines 1~3**: Actions will be triggered by the on(Release) event (i.e., a mouse click).
**Line 2**: Rotates the position of the fish_mc movie clip by 5 degrees counterclockwise.

6 The Rotate Decrease button contains the following actions.

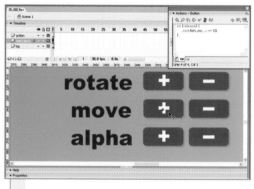

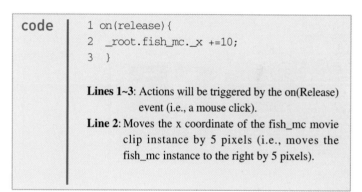

```
code    1 on(release){
        2 _root.fish_mc._x +=10;
        3 }
```

**Lines 1~3**: Actions will be triggered by the on(Release) event (i.e., a mouse click).
**Line 2**: Moves the x coordinate of the fish_mc movie clip instance by 5 pixels (i.e., moves the fish_mc instance to the right by 5 pixels).

7 Add the following actions to the Move Increase button.

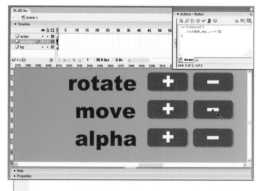

```
code    1 on(release){
        2 _root.fish_mc._x -=10;
        3 }
```

**Lines 1~3**: Actions will be triggered by the on(Release) event (i.e., a mouse click).
**Line 2**: Moves the x coordinate of the fish_mc movie clip instance by 5 pixels to the left.

8 Add the following actions to the Move Decrease button.

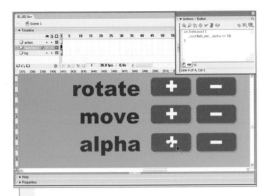

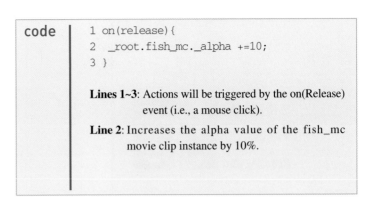

```
code
1 on(release){
2   _root.fish_mc._alpha +=10;
3 }
```

**Lines 1~3**: Actions will be triggered by the on(Release) event (i.e., a mouse click).

**Line 2**: Increases the alpha value of the fish_mc movie clip instance by 10%.

9 The Alpha Value Increase button contains the following actions.

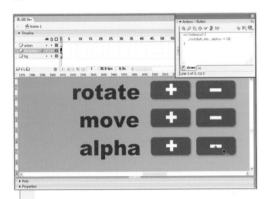

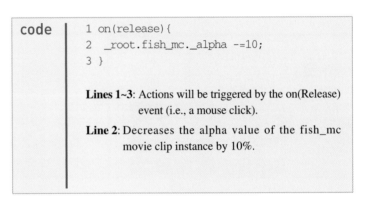

```
code
1 on(release){
2   _root.fish_mc._alpha -=10;
3 }
```

**Lines 1~3**: Actions will be triggered by the on(Release) event (i.e., a mouse click).

**Line 2**: Decreases the alpha value of the fish_mc movie clip instance by 10%.

10 The Alpha Value Decrease button contains the following actions.

11 Test the movie and click the buttons to check that the fish_mc movie clip instance properties change.

# 3 Making a Floating Menu Panel

In this example, you will use the startDrag() and stopDrag() actions to create a movie clip that behaves like a floating menu panel. By the end of this exercise, you will be able to drag the panel around using the blue bar at the top.

**Start File**
\Sample\Chapter05\05_003.fla

**Final File**
\Sample\Chapter05\05_003_end.fla

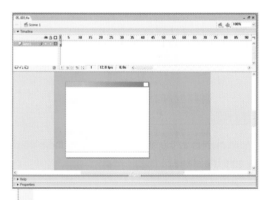

1 Open the start file. You should see a movie clip instance that is shaped like a menu panel.

**note >>**

The information used by an action is called an argument. Arguments may be required or optional. In this example, the name of the target movie clip instance is a required argument for the startDrag() action.

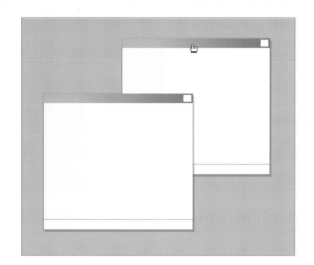

2 To make every instance of the menu panel draggable, you will add the ActionScript to the library symbol. Any movie clip instances will inherit these actions. Open the Library panel and double-click the [Menu Movie Clip] symbol to enter editing mode.

3 The movie clip symbol is composed of three layers—shadow, top_menu, and close_menu.

**code**

```
1  on(press){
2  startDrag(this, false) ;
3  }
4  on(release){
5  stopDrag();
6  }
```

**Lines 1~3**: Actions will be triggered by the onPress event (i.e., holding down the mouse button).

**Line 2**: The startDrag() action turns on dragging for the movie clip. The word **this** refers to the current movie clip (**menu**), which includes the button. Using the word **false** causes the dragging to occur from the point at which the instance was clicked.

**Lines 4~6**: Actions will be triggered by the onRelease event (i.e., upon releasing the button).

**Line 5**: Stops the dragging of the movie clip that has the startDrag() action command applied.

|4| Click the top_menu layer and select the blue-colored top panel. The Property Inspector will show that it is an instance of the t-menu button.

|5| Press [F9] to open the Actions panel. In the Actions panel, enter the startDrag() and stopDrag() action commands shown above. These actions will cause the panel to move when dragged by the mouse, and stop when released.

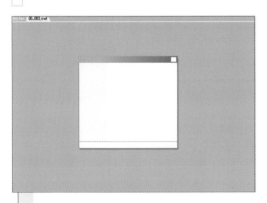

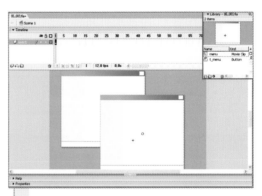

|6| Test the animation by pressing [Ctrl]-[Enter]. You should be able to drag the panel using the blue bar at the top of the menu.

|7| You can add more menus to the stage by dragging them from the Library window onto the stage.

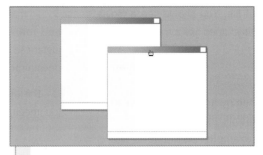

|8| Run Test Movie again to test each of the selected menu panels.

# Using the fscommand to Execute an External Program

In this example, you will learn to use the fscommand to open two Windows programs–Notepad and Windows Explorer.

┌─ **Start File**
  ● \Sample\Chapter05\05_004.fla

┌─ **Final File**
  ● \Sample\Chapter05\05_004_end.fla

┌ **Executable Files**
  ● \Sample\Chapter05\ fscommand \ explorer.exe
  ● \Sample\Chapter05\ fscommand \notepad.exe

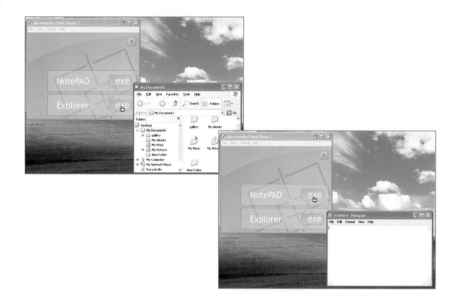

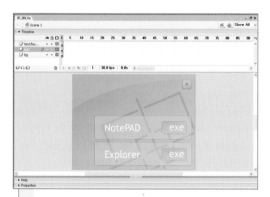

1 Open the start file. You will see that it contains buttons for starting and stopping Notepad and Windows Explorer.

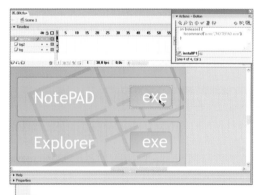

2 Select the Notepad button instance and press [F9] to open the Actions panel. When the Start button is selected in the Actions panel, enter the actions shown here.

**tip >>**

### fscommand exec Command

This command is used to open a program. Programs that will be opened must be stored in an fscommand folder within the current folder.

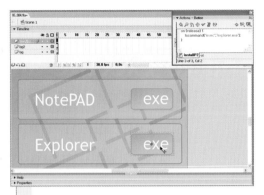

```
code    1   on(release){
        2   fscommand("exec","explorer.exe");
        3   }
```

**Lines 1~3**: Actions will be triggered by the on(Release) event (i.e., clicking the mouse button).

**Line 2**: The "exec" command will open the **Explorer.exe** file.

3 Repeat the steps above to define the action for **Explorer.exe** on the Explorer button.

```
code    1   on(release){
        2   fscommand("quit");
        3   }
```

**Lines 1~3**: Actions will be triggered by the on(Release) event (i.e., clicking the mouse button).

**Line 2**: The "quit" command will close the Flash Player.

4 Let's add the quit command to the Close button in the top-right corner so that it can be used to close the Flash Player. Click the close instance, open the Actions panel, and enter the fscommand in the sidebar to the right.

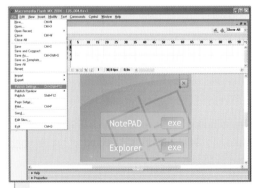

5 Select [File] - [Save] to save your work and open the Publish Settings dialog box by selecting [File] - [Publish Settings].

tip >>
**exec Command**

You cannot test the "exec" fscommand() command within Flash. You need to either create a Flash project file (EXE) or open the Flash movie file (SWF) in the standalone Flash Player.

6 | Select [Windows Projector(.exe)] to create the Projector File. You will see that the Projector file (EXE) is given the same name as the file.

7 | Click the [Publish] button to create the Projector file. Open the folder containing the original Flash file and locate the Projector file ( ). Double-click to open this file. You should be able to click on the Notepad and Explorer buttons to run each of these programs. Click the button at the top-right corner of the file to quit the Flash Player.

You can also double-click to open the movie in the Flash Player. The buttons should work in exactly the same way as described for the EXE file.

# Creating ActionScript with the Behaviors Panel

The Behaviors panel is another way to add ActionScript to a Flash movie. Behaviors are common actions that can be applied to Flash objects. To add a behavior, select the behavior from the Behaviors panel, enter some settings, and the actions will be added to your movie automatically. Behaviors can also be linked to specific events, such as a mouse click. In this example, you will use the Behaviors panel to add actions to Play and Stop buttons within a movie.

**Start File**
• \Sample\Chapter05\05_005.fla

**Final File**
• \Sample\Chapter05\05_005_end.fla

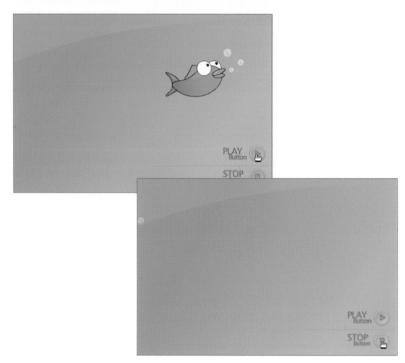

1 Open the start file. It contains a moving fish animation with buttons to play and stop the animation in the right-hand corner of the screen. Preview the movie by pressing [Ctrl]-[Enter]. The animation loops continuously without stopping.

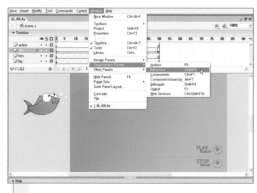

2 Select [Window] - [Development Panels] - [Behaviors] or use the shortcut keys [Shift]-[F3] to open the Behaviors panel.

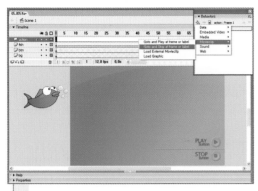

3  The animation will be paused at the beginning, and we will control it using the Play and Stop buttons. Add a stop action to frame 1 of the action layer by selecting the frame in the timeline and clicking the [Add Behavior] icon (⊞) in the Behaviors panel. Select [Movieclip] - [Goto And Stop at frame or label] from the menu.

4  In the Goto and Stop at frame or label dialog box, press [OK] to apply the default values.

5  If you press [F9] to open the Actions panel, you will see that a gotoAndStop() action has been entered into frame 1 of the action layer automatically. You will also see the action listed within the Behaviors panel.

6  Press [Ctrl]-[Enter] to test the movie. The animation should be stopped.

7  Select the Play button instance and use the [Add Behavior] icon (⊞) to select the [Movieclip] - [Goto And Play at frame or label] behavior.

8  Enter frame 2 at the bottom of the dialog box and press [OK].

207

9  If you open the Actions panel, you will see that an onRelease event has been added. When the Play button is clicked, the movie clip will move to frame 2 and play.

10  Select the Stop button. In the Behaviors panel, click the [Add Behavior] icon (⊞) and choose [Movieclip] - [Goto And Stop at frame or label]. Press [OK] to accept the default value.

11  In the Actions panel, you will see an on(Release) event that moves to frame 1 and stops playing the movie.

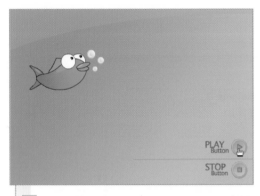

12  Press [Ctrl]-[Enter] to test the movie. Click the buttons to make sure that the animation works correctly.

# 6 Using Behaviors to Control Movie Clips

Behaviors can be used to control the way a movie clip plays, as well as the way it is displayed on the stage. In this example, you will use behaviors with movie clips to create draggable panels.

**Start File**
\Sample\Chapter05\05_006.fla

**Final File**
\Sample\Chapter05\05_006_end.fla

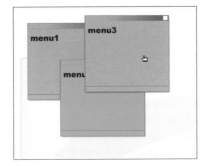
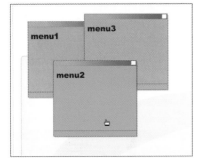

1 The start file contains only a basic background design on the stage. Press [F11] to open the Library panel.

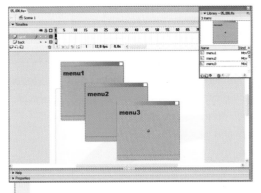

2 Drag the menu1, menu2, and menu3 movie clips onto the stage and position them as shown above.

3 In the Property Inspector, enter **menu1_mc**, **menu2_mc,** and **menu3_mc** as instance names for each of the instances.

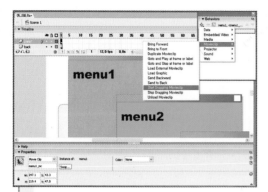

**4** Let's make each of the movie clip instances draggable on the stage. Select the menu1_mc movie clip instance, go to the Behaviors panel, and select [Movieclip] - [Start Dragging Movieclip].

**5** In the Start Dragging Movieclip dialog box, make sure the Relative option is chosen and that menu1_mc is selected as the draggable movie clip instance.

**6** The Start Dragging Movieclip action should be activated while the mouse is held down on the panel. In the Behaviors panel, change the Event to [On Press].

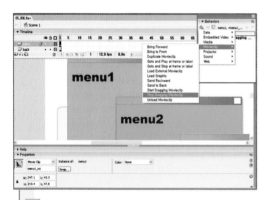

**7** To stop the movement of the panel, select the menu1_mc movie clip instance and go to the Behaviors panel. Select [MovieClip] - [Stop Dragging Movieclip] and click [OK].

**8** Repeat the steps above for the menu2_mc and menu3_mc movie clip instances.

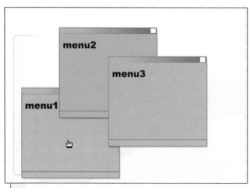

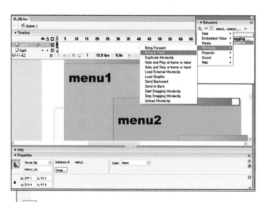

**9** Press [Ctrl]-[Enter] to test the movie. Make sure you can drag each movie clip instance.

**10** Next, let's make a movie clip come to the front when selected. Click the menu1_mc instance and select [Movieclip] - [Bring to Front] in the Behaviors panel.

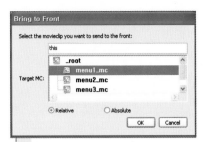

**11** In the Bring to Front dialog box, make sure the Relative option and menu1_mc instance are selected.

**12** The Bring to Front action needs to be applied while the mouse is pressed on the button. In the Behaviors panel change the Bring to Front Event to [On Press].

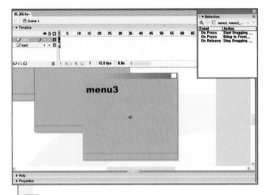

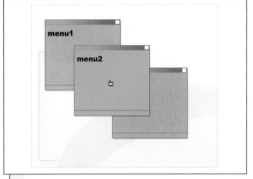

**13** Repeat the steps above to define Bring to Front behaviors for the menu2_mc and menu3_mc movie clip instances. Make sure that the events for these two movie clip instances are changed to [On Press]

**14** Press [Ctrl]-[Enter] to test the movie. When you drag each panel, it will move to the front of the other panels.

*Exercise*

# 7

# Creating a Photo Gallery with Behaviors

In this example, you will use the [MovieClip] - [Load Graphic] behavior to create a photo gallery viewer. This method is useful for keeping down the file size of your Flash movies because images are only loaded if needed.

**Start File**
- \Sample\Chapter05\05_007.fla

**Final File**
- \Sample\Chapter05\05_007_end.fla

**Import Files**
- \Sample\Chapter05\image\pic1.jpg
- \Sample\Chapter05\image\pic2.jpg
- \Sample\Chapter05\image\pic3.jpg

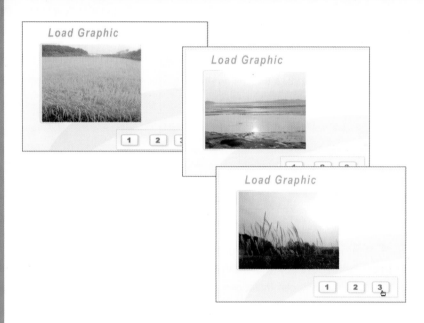

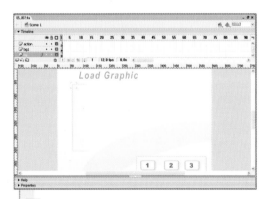

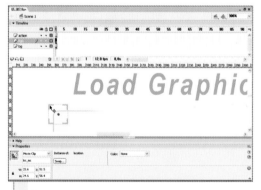

1 Open the start file. The movie contains three buttons and a movie clip instance that will be used as a container for the JPEG images.

2 Select the location movie clip symbol from the top-left corner.

3 Enter the instance name **loc_mc** in the Property Inspector.

212

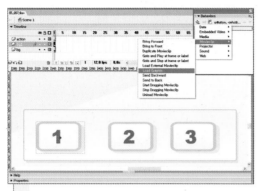

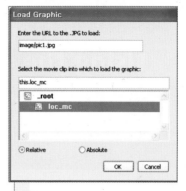

4 Select the button labeled 1 at the bottom-right corner of the stage. Select [MovieClip] - [Load Graphic] from the Behaviors panel. The Load Graphic dialog box will open.

5 Enter the URL **image/pic1.jpg** in the [Enter the URL to the .JPG to load] section. Select loc_mc in the [Select the movie clip into which to load the graphic] section.

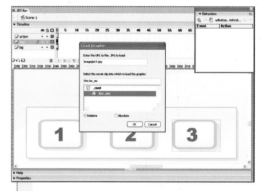

6 Select the second button, select [Load Graphic] from the Behaviors panel, and enter the settings **image/pic2.jpg** and loc_mc.

7 Select the third button, go to the Behaviors panel, and enter the settings **img/pic3.jpg** and loc_mc.

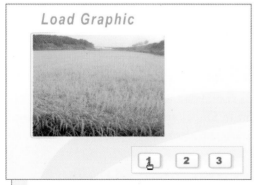

8 Press [Ctrl]-[Enter] to test the movie. Click each of the three buttons to make sure that the relevant images load.

*Exercise*

# 8

# Using the Embedded Video Behavior

In this exercise, we will import a video clip and add actions to buttons that will play, pause, stop, show, and hide the clip.

**Start File**
- \Sample\Chapter05\05_008.fla

**Final File**
- \Sample\Chapter05\05_008_end.fla

**Import Files**
- \Sample\Chapter05\video \SampleVideo1.avi

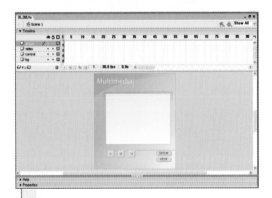

**1** Open the start file. It contains play, pause, stop, show, and hide buttons that will be used to control playback of an imported video clip.

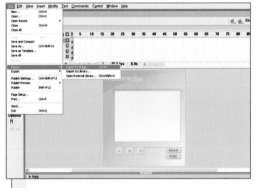

**2** Click the video layer. Insert the video clip by selecting [File] - [Import] - [Import to Stage] and choosing the file **Sample\ Chapter05\video\SampleVideo1.avi**.

3 Press the [Next] and then [Finish] buttons without making changes to the settings in the Video Import dialog box.

4 If you are prompted to add frames, click the [Yes] button.

tip >>

### Positioning the Video Clip

You can either drag the video clip instance to the correct position on the stage or use the Info panel to enter coordinates. The position can also be set using the X and Y coordinates in the Property Inspector.

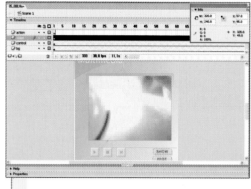

5 Select the video clip instance and open the Info panel using the [Ctrl]-[I] shortcut keys. Click the top-left XY position in the center of the panel and set the coordinates to X: 57 and Y: 95.

6 Select frame 333 of the control and bg layers and press the [F5] button to add frames.

7 Select the video clip instance on the video layer and set the instance name to sample_video in the Property Inspector.

8 The movie should stop at frame 1 so that the video clip doesn't play automatically. Click frame 1 of the action layer and click the [Add Behavior] icon () in the Behaviors panel. Select [MovieClip] - [Goto and Stop at frame or label].

9 Click [OK] to accept the default settings in the Goto and Stop at frame or label dialog box.

10 Select the Play button and choose [Add Behavior (⊕)] - [Embedded Video] - [Play] from the Behaviors panel.

11 Choose sample_video to specify the clip to play when the Play button is clicked. Click [OK].

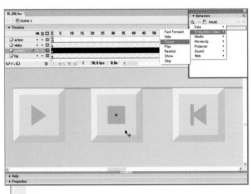

12 Select the Pause button and select [Add Behavior (⊕)] - [Embedded Video] - [Pause] from the Behaviors panel.

13 Choose sample_video and click [OK].

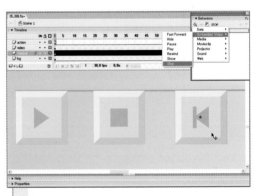

14 Select the Stop button and select [Add Behavior (⊕)] - [Embedded Video] - [Stop] from the Behaviors panel.

15 Choose sample_video and click [OK].

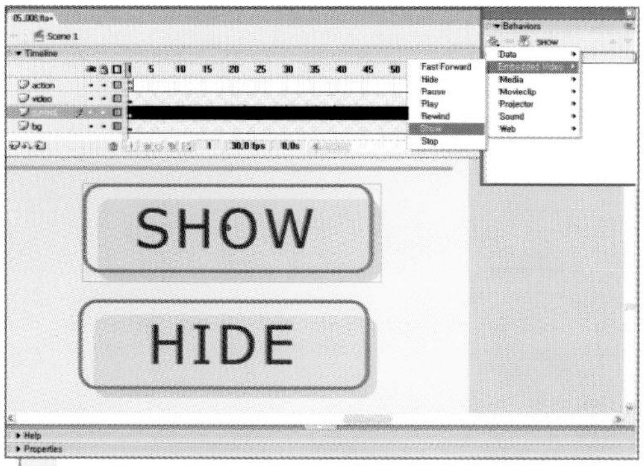


16 Select the Show button and click [Add Behavior ()] - [Embedded Video] - [Show] in the Behaviors panel. Choose sample_video and click [OK].

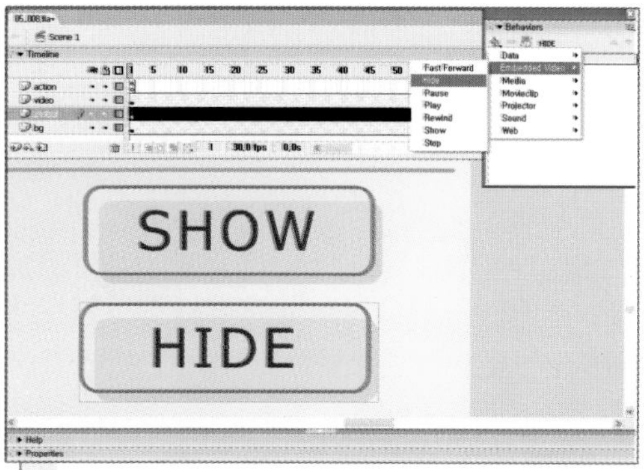


17 Select the Hide button and select [Add Behavior ()] - [Embedded Video] - [Hide] in the Behaviors panel. Choose sample_video and click [OK].

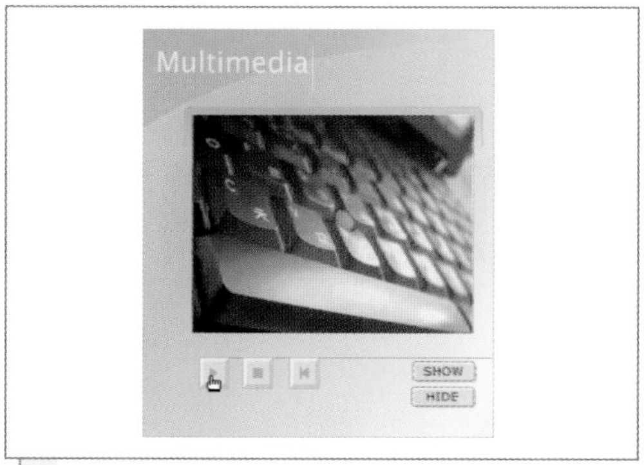


18 Test the movie using [Ctrl]-[Enter]. Click each button to see the effect on the sample_video video clip instance.

Chapter | 6

# Advanced Animation Techniques

So far, you have learned to use simple animation techniques to create Flash movies. However, you can create more complicated animations by working with movie clip symbols. Movie clip symbols have their own timeline, which means they are like small Flash movies placed within the main movie. A movie clip symbol plays independently of any animation that occurs on the main timeline.

# Using Movie Clips and Templates

Movie clip symbols allow you to include the same animation at several different places within your movie. In this section, you will learn more about movie clip symbols. You will also learn to import video files as well as create and use Flash templates.

## Movie Clip Symbols

Movie clip symbols run within their own timeline, which is completely separate from the main timeline. You can create movie clip symbols using exactly the same animation techniques that you have learned so far. Each movie clip symbol can also be controlled by coding with behaviors and ActionScript.

One advantage of using movie clip symbols is that the symbols can be reused throughout the Flash movie. No matter how many times it appears, a movie clip is stored once, so your overall file size will be unchanged. Video clips can also be inserted as movie clip symbols.

## Working with Video

Although you can create animations from scratch in Flash, you can also import files-including video files-in a variety of different formats and include them in your animation.

By default, Flash uses the Sorenson Spark Codec to compress files for export. The same codec is used to decompress files for viewing on a user's computer. 'Codec' literally means compression and decompression. The process reduces file sizes but files also lose quality with each compression.

**For expanded video capabilities, see Sorenson Spark Pro**
**www.sorenson.com/sparkpro**

```
All Video Formats
All PostScript (*.AI;*.PDF;*.EPS)
FreeHand (*.fh*;*.ft*)
PNG File (*.png)
Adobe Illustrator (*.eps,*.ai)
AutoCAD DXF (*.dxf)
Bitmap (*.bmp,*.dib)
Enhanced Metafile (*.emf)
Flash Movie (*.swf,*.spl)
GIF Image (*.gif)
JPEG Image (*.jpg)
Windows Metafile (*.wmf)
Macintosh PICT Image (*.pct)
MacPaint Image (*.pntg)
PhotoShop 2.5, 3 Image (*.psd)
QuickTime Image (*.qtif)
Silicon Graphics Image (*.sgi)
TGA Image (*.tga)
TIFF Image (*.tif,*.tiff)
WAV Sound (*.wav)
MP3 Sound (*.mp3)
AIFF Sound (*.aif)
Sun AU (*.au)
QuickTime Movie (*.mov)
Video for Windows (*.avi)
MPEG Movie (*.mpg,*.mpeg)
Digital Video (*.dv,*.dvi)
Windows Media (*.asf,*.wmv)
Macromedia Flash Video (*.flv)
All Files (*.*)
```

The Import dialog box lists the file formats supported by Flash.

# Importing Video Files

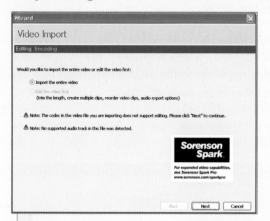

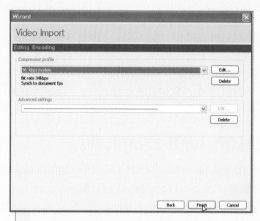

**1** Choose [File] - [Import] - [Import to Stage] or [File] - [Import] - [Import to Library] to open the Import dialog box. Select the video file to import and click [OK]. In the Video Import Wizard dialog box, choose your import options and click [Finish].

**2** In the Video Import Wizard dialog box, you can choose to import the entire video, or edit it first.

**3** When the [Import the entire video] option is selected, the Editing Encoding option will appear. This is used to set the compression rate and file settings.

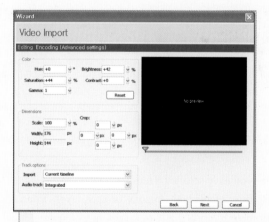

**4** Clicking the [Edit] button beside [Compression profile] brings up the window pictured above.

**5** Under [Advanced settings], choose [Create new profile...] to open the window above. This window is used to change video file options such as color, size, and sound. You will have the option to turn the video into a movie clip before it is imported.

Templates are movies that have already been set up with symbols and frames. Templates allow people to share a common Flash file structure. For example, a company could set up a standard template file for their corporate presentations that includes the company logo. Any employee within the company could then use the template and add content as required. Flash includes a number of pre-made templates.

## Working with Templates

Select [File] - [New] to open the New Document dialog box, then click the [Templates] tab. Select a category and choose the appropriate template. You will see a preview on the right of the dialog box.

You can also select the template category from the [Create from Template] area of the start page.

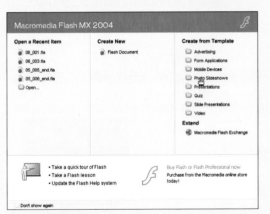

After you have selected a template, familiarize yourself with the contents and structure of each layer. You can customize layers and add new content as required. You can also insert additional frames and keyframes, depending on the way the template is structured.

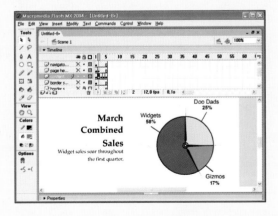

# Creating a Bouncing Ball Movie Clip

In this section, you will learn to create a movie clip symbol that includes a bouncing ball animation. You will also animate the movie clip symbol on the main timeline. In effect, you will be creating a double animation.

**Start File**
\Sample\Chapter06\06_001.fla

**Final File**
\Sample\Chapter06\06_001_end.fla

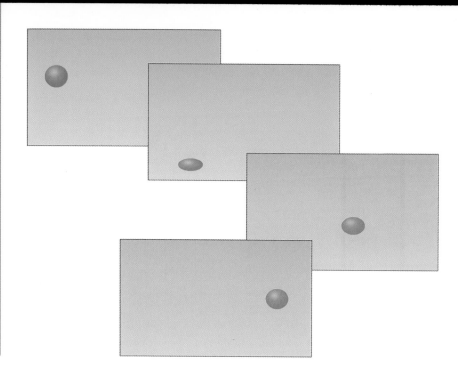

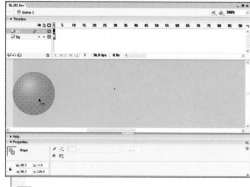

1 Open the start file and select the Shape object in the ani layer.

2 Press the [F8] key to open the Convert to Symbol dialog box. Set the name to **ball**, the behavior to Movie Clip, and click [OK].

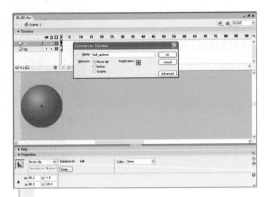

3 Select the ball symbol on the stage and press [F8]. In the Convert to Symbol dialog box, enter the name **ball_updown**, set the behavior to Movie Clip, and click [OK].

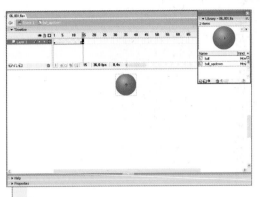

4 Double-click the ball_updown symbol to enter Symbol Edit mode. Select frame 15 on Layer 1 and press [F6] to insert a keyframe.

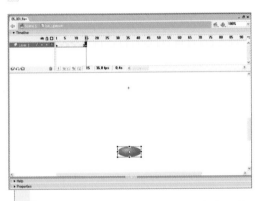

5 At frame 15, move the ball symbol to the bottom of the stage and use the Free Transform tool (⊞) to shorten and widen the ball as shown above.

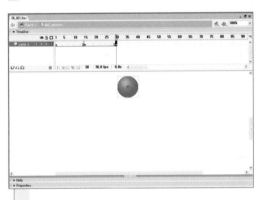

6 Select frame 1 of Layer 1, hold down the [Alt] key, and drag the keyframe to frame 30.

7 Select frames 1 through 29, right-click, and select [Create Motion Tween] from the shortcut menu. Click Scene 1 to return to the main timeline.

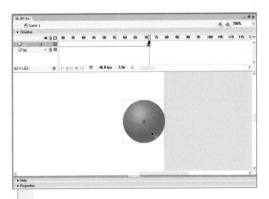

8 Select frame 72 of the ani layer and press [F6] to insert a keyframe. Hold down the [Shift] key and move the ball_updown symbol to the right edge of the stage as shown above.

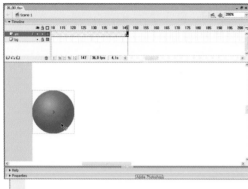

You could have also copied frame 1 of the ani layer and pasted it into frame 147.

9 Select frame 147 of the ani layer and press [F6] to insert a keyframe. Hold down the [Shift] key and move the ball_updown symbol to the left edge of the stage as shown above.

10 Select frame 147 of the bg layer and press [F5] to insert frames. Motion tween frames 1 through 146 of the ani layer.

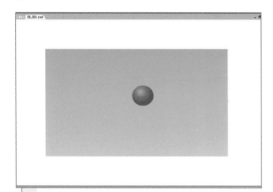

11 Press [Ctrl]-[Enter] to test the movie.

*Exercise*

# 2

# Importing Video Clips into Movie Clips

Video can be imported into movie clip symbols. Each time we duplicate the movie clip symbol that contains the video, the file size of the Flash movie file will be unaffected. When a video is contained within a movie clip symbol, it can also be animated and manipulated with ActionScript. In this section, we will add a video clip to a movie clip symbol and apply a color value.

**Start File**
\Sample\Chapter06\06_002.fla

**Final File**
\Sample\Chapter06\06_002_end.fla

**Import File**
\Sample\Chapter06\video\asd.wmv

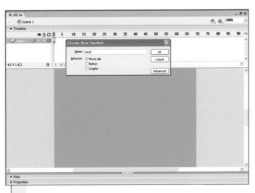

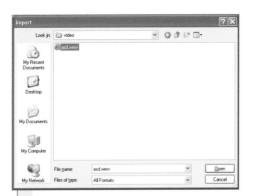

[1] Open the start file. Press [Ctrl]-[F8] to open the Create New Symbol dialog box. Set the name to **mov**, the behavior to Movie Clip, and click [OK].

[2] Select [File] - [Import] - [Import to Stage], choose video/asd.wmv, and click [Open].

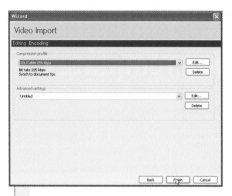

It can take a long time to import a video file, depending on the speed of your computer. If importing takes too long, click the [Cancel] button and work with the final resource file.

**3** Press [Next] to import the entire video and click [Finish].

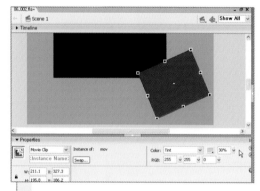

**4** If you are prompted to add frames to the timeline in order to display the video's entire length, click [Yes].

**5** After importing the video, click Scene 1 to return to the main timeline. Press [Ctrl]-[L] to open the Library panel, select the mov movie clip symbol, and drag it onto the stage.

**6** Select the mov movie clip symbol and drag it while holding down the [Alt] key. This will duplicate the movie clip. Use the Free Transform tool ( ) to make the duplicate smaller and rotate it as shown above.

**7** Open the Property Inspector and set the color style to tint, the color to #FFFF00, and the tint amount to 30%.

**8** Press [Ctrl]-[Enter] to test the movie.

# 3

# Making Your Own Templates

The templates provided within Flash can help to speed up the process of creating a movie. In this section, you'll explore how you can create your own templates.

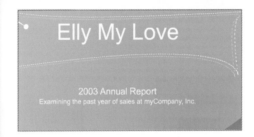

**Start File**
\Sample\Chapter06\06_003.fla

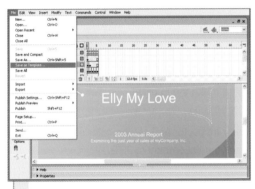

1 Open the start file and select [File] - [Save as Template].

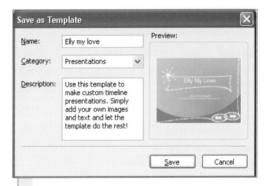

2 Set the name to **Elly My Love**, the category to Presentations, and click [Save].

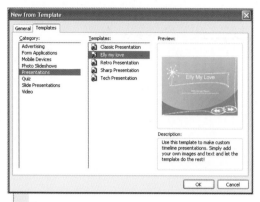

3 The template has now been registered in Flash. Close the movie file and press [Ctrl]-[N] to create a new movie. Choose the [Templates] tab and select the Presentations category. You should see the Elly My Love template in the list.

# Adding Movie Clips to Buttons

Movie clips can be added to buttons so that they animate according to the movement of the mouse. In this section, you will add an animation to a menu button.

**Start File**
\Sample\Chapter06\06_004.fla

**Final File**
\Sample\Chapter06\06_004_end.fla

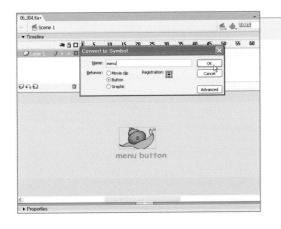

1  Open the start file. Select all objects on the stage and press [F8] to open the Convert to Symbol dialog box. Enter the name **menu**, set the behavior to Button, and press [OK].

2  Double-click the button symbol to enter the Symbol Edit mode. Select the Up frame of Layer 1 and press [F6] twice to insert keyframes into the Over and Down frames. Select the Hit frame and press [F7] to insert a blank frame.

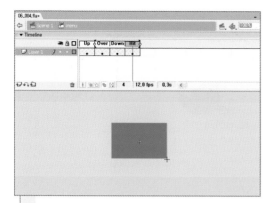

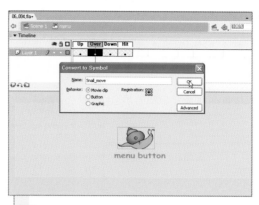

3 Click the [Edit Multiple Frames] icon in the timeline and use the Rectangle tool (▢) to draw the rectangle shown here. This rectangle will become the button's selection area. Click the [Edit Multiple Frames] icon (▤) to return to single frame editing.

4 Click the Over frame and select the Snail symbol. Press [F8] to open the Convert to Symbol dialog box. Enter the name **Snail_move**, the behavior Movie Clip, and press [OK].

5 Select the menu button text in the Over frame and change the color to #CC6633.

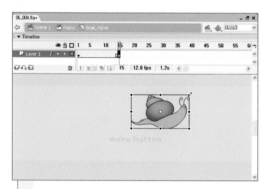

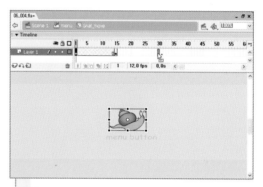

6 Double-click the Snail_move symbol to enter Symbol Edit mode. Select frame 15 and press [F6] to insert a keyframe. Use the Free Transform tool (▣) to make the symbol larger, then move it slightly to the right.

7 Select frame 1, hold down [Alt], and drag it to frame 30.

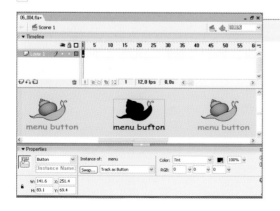

8 Click Scene 1 of the timeline to return to the main timeline. Hold down the [Alt] key and drag to create three copies of the symbol.

9 Select the symbol in the center and set the color style to Tint and the color to #000000 in the Property Inspector. Set the tint percentage to 100%.

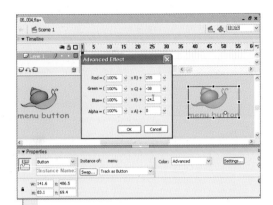

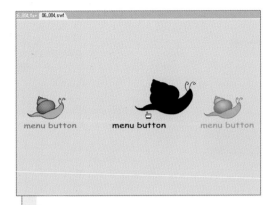

**10** Select the symbol on the right and set the color style to Advanced in the Property Inspector. Next, click the [Settings] button.

**11** In the Advanced Effect dialog box, set R)+: **255**, G)+: **-38**, B)+: **-24**, and click [OK].

**12** Press [Ctrl]-[Enter] to test the movie. Click each of the buttons to test their effects.

# 5 Using Actions to Control Movie Clips

It is common to use Flash to make menus for Web sites because Flash allows menus to be animated. In this section, you will create a simple menu that is animated using movie clip symbols.

**Start File**
  \Sample\Chapter06\06_005.fla

**Final File**
  \Sample\Chapter06\06_005_end.fla

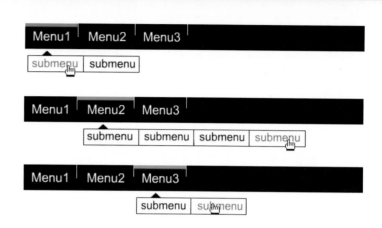

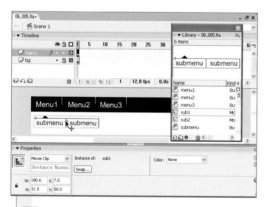

1 Open the start file. Press [Ctrl]-[L] to open the Library panel and place the sub1 movie clip symbol below Menu1.

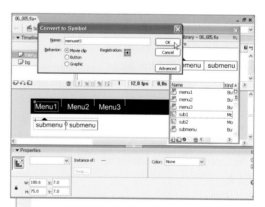

2 Select both Menu1 and the sub1 symbol and press [F8]. Enter the name **menuset1** and choose the Movie Clip behavior before clicking [OK].

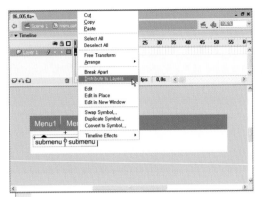

3 Double-click menuset1 to enter Symbol-Editing mode. Select the sub1 symbol, right-click, and select [Distribute to Layers] from the shortcut menu.

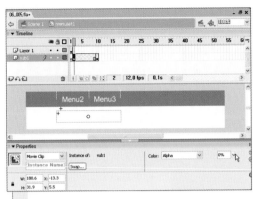

4 Select frame 1 of the sub1 layer, move it to frame 2, and insert a keyframe at frame 10.

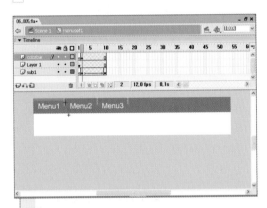

5 Select frame 2 of the sub1 layer, move the sub1 symbol to the right, and set the alpha value to 0%.

6 Motion tween frames 2 to 9 of the sub1 layer. Select Layer 1 and click the [Insert Layer] icon ( ) to insert a new layer. Change the layer name to **colorbar** and insert a keyframe into frame 2.

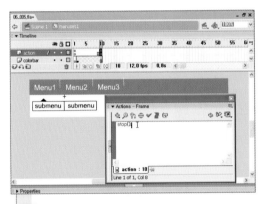

7 Use the Rectangle tool ( ) to draw the rectangle as shown here—using a fill color of #FF3399 and no line color. Click frame 10 of Layer 1 and press [F5] to add frames.

8 Select the colorbar layer and click the [Insert Layer] icon ( ) to insert a new layer. Name the new layer **action** and insert keyframes at frames 1 and 10.

9 Let's insert the stop(); action into each keyframe. In the Actions - Frames panel, click on the [Add a New Item to the Script] button and select [Global Functions] - [Timeline Control] - [Stop].

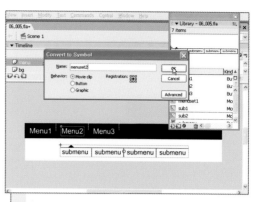

**10** Click Scene 1 to return to the main timeline. From the Library panel, drag the sub2 movie clip symbol and place it below Menu2.

**11** Select both the Menu2 and sub2 symbols and press [F8]. Enter the name **menuset2** and set the behavior to Movie Clip. Click [OK].

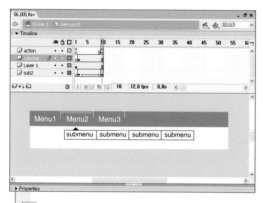

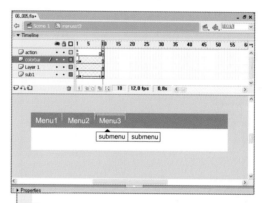

**12** Repeat steps 3 to 9 above to create the menuset2 movie clip. The color of the colorbar rectangle should be #66CC00.

**13** Repeat steps 3 to 9 to make the menuset3 movie clip. The color of the colorbar rectangle should be #3399FF.

14 In the main timeline, select each of the symbols and enter an instance name in the Property Inspector. Name them as follows: **menu1, menu2,** and **menu3.**

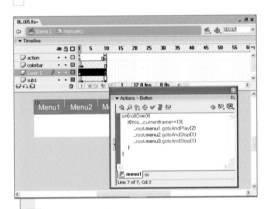

15 Double-click the menuset1 symbol to enter Symbol Edit mode. Select the menu1 button symbol and enter the actions as shown.

code
```
1  on(rollOver){
2      if(this._currentframe==1){
3          _root.menu1.gotoAndPlay(2)
4          _root.menu2.gotoAndStop(1)
5          _root.menu3.gotoAndStop(1)
6      }
7  }
```

**Line 1**: Actions will be triggered by the onRollover event (i.e., the mouse is moved over the button).
**Line 2**: If the current frame of this movie clip is frame 1,
**Line 3**: Go to frame 2 in the menu1 instance and play.
**Line 4**: Go to frame 1 in the menu2 instance and stop.
**Line 5**: Go to frame 1 in the menu3 instance and stop.

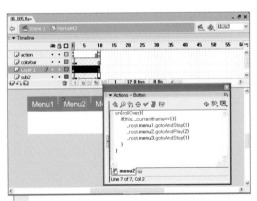

16 Return to the main stage. Double-click the menuset2 symbol to enter Symbol Edit mode, select the menu2 button symbol, and enter the actions shown here.

code
```
1  on(rollOver){
2      if(this._currentframe==1){
3          _root.menu1.gotoAndStop(1)
4          _root.menu2.gotoAndPlay(2)
5          _root.menu3.gotoAndStop(1)
6      }
7  }
```

**Line 1**: Actions will be triggered by the onRollover event (i.e., the mouse is moved over the button).
**Line 2**: If the current frame of this movie clip is frame 1,
**Line 3**: Go to frame 1 in the menu1 instance and stop.
**Line 4**: Go to frame 2 in the menu2 instance and play.
**Line 5**: Go to frame 1 in the menu3 instance and stop.

**17** Return to the main stage. Double-click the menuset3 symbol, select the menu3 button symbol, and enter the actions shown here.

**18** Press [Ctrl]-[Enter] to test the movie. Move the mouse over each of the menu buttons to ensure that they work correctly.

**code**

```
1   on(rollOver){
2     if(this._currentframe==1){
3       _root.menu1.gotoAndStop(1)
4       _root.menu2.gotoAndStop(1)
5       _root.menu3.gotoAndPlay(2)
6     }
7   }
```

**Line 1**: Actions will be triggered by the onRollover event (i.e., the mouse is moved over the button).

**Line 2**: If the current frame of this movie clip is frame 1,

**Line 3**: Go to frame 1 in the menu1 instance and stop.

**Line 4**: Go to frame 1 in the menu2 instance and stop.

**Line 5**: Go to frame 2 in the menu3 instance and play.

# 6 Using Masks and Movie Clips to Make an Ad Movie

This example uses a mask on a bitmap image to create an animated background for a Flash advertisement.

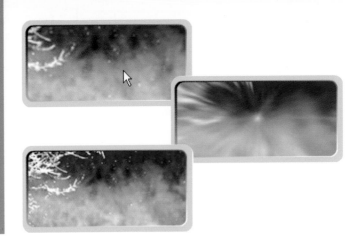

**Start File**
 \Sample\Chapter06\06_006.fla

**Final File**
 \Sample\Chapter06\06_006_end.fla

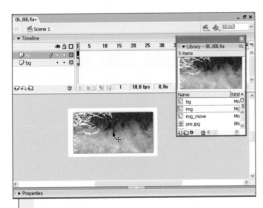

1 Open the start file and select the ani layer. Open the Library panel and drag the img symbol onto the stage.

2 Select the img movie clip symbol, press [F8], and create the mov movie clip symbol.

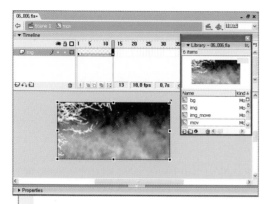

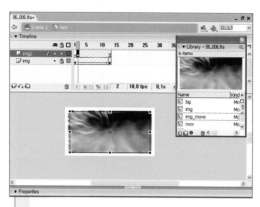

3 Double-click the mov movie clip symbol. Change the name of the Layer 1 layer to **img**. Insert a keyframe at frame 13. Use the Free Transform tool to increase the size of the image and add a motion tween to frames 1 through 13.

4 Select the img layer, insert a new layer, and name it **img2**. Open the Library panel and drag the img_move movie clip symbol into the img2 layer. Drag frame 1 of the img2 layer to frame 2.

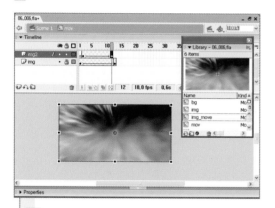

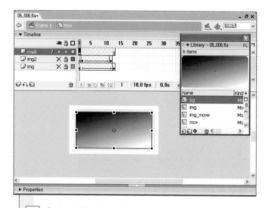

5 Insert a keyframe at frame 12 of the img2 layer. Increase the size of the img_move symbol and motion tween frames 2 through 11. Select frame 13 and delete it with the [Shift]-[F5] shortcut.

6 Select the img2 layer and insert a new layer. Name the layer **mask**. Lock and hide the img and img2 layers. Open the Library panel and drag the bg movie clip symbol onto the stage. Line it up with the image on the stage.

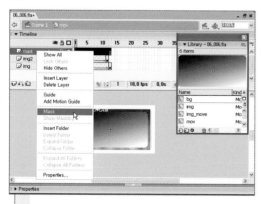

7 Right-click the mask layer and select [Mask] from the shortcut menu.

8 To mask the img layer, drag it towards the img2 layer. The layer should appear indented underneath the mask layer.

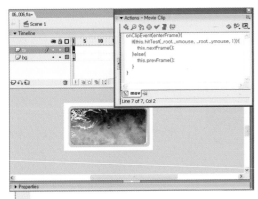

```
code    1  onClipEvent(enterFrame){
        2    if(this.hitTest(_root._xmouse,
             _root._ymouse, 1)){
        3      this.nextFrame();
        4    }else{
        5      this.prevFrame();
        6    }
        7  }
```

**Line 1**: Actions will be triggered when the frame of the movie clip is entered.

**Line 2**: If the mouse is placed on top of the movie clip,

**Line 3**: Go to the next frame and play.

**Line 4**: If not,

**Line 5**: Go to the previous frame and play.

9 Return to the main stage. Select the mov movie clip symbol and press [F9] to open the Actions panel. Enter the following ActionScript.

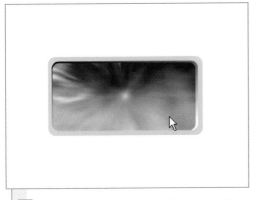

10 Press [Ctrl]-[Enter] to test the movie. Move the mouse over and out of the image to watch the effect.

240

# PDF and EPS File Support

Flash MX 2004 allows you to import PDF and EPS files. The PDF file format is used for document sharing while EPS files are mainly used for printing. Flash provides you with a number of options when you import these file types.

You can import a file using either [File] - [Import] - [Import to Stage] or [File] - [Import] - [Import to Library]. Either option will open the Import dialog box. Select the PDF or EPS file to import and click [OK]. This will open the Import Options dialog box shown below.

## Import Options Dialog Box

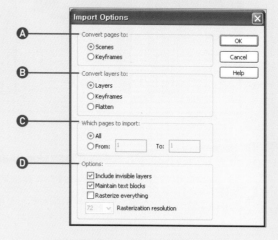

### Ⓐ Convert pages to:

This option allows you to determine whether each page will be imported into a separate scene or into a separate keyframe.

### Ⓑ Convert layers to:

The Convert Layers option allows you to specify how each layer will be imported: Layers, Keyframes, or Flatten.

### Ⓒ Which pages to import:

Selecting [All] will import all pages. You can also specify the page numbers to import.

### Ⓓ Options:

- Include invisible layers: All hidden layers will be imported.
- Maintain text blocks: Text blocks will be preserved after importing.
- Rasterize everything: When this option is checked, the imported content will be rasterized (i.e., converted into bitmaps). You will be able to select the resolution.

PDF (Portable Document Format) files are created and read using Adobe Acrobat. However, it is possible to work with PDF files in Flash MX 2004.

**Final File**
- \Sample\Chapter06 \06_007_end.fla

**Import File**
- \Sample\Chapter06\files \pdfSample.pdf

# Loading PDF Files into Flash

*01* The image below shows the PDF sample file viewed in Adobe Acrobat. This file has five pages.

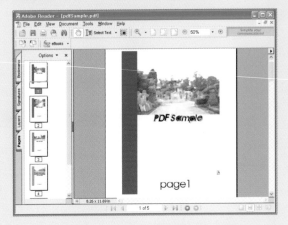

*02* Press [Ctrl]-[N], select [Flash Document], and click [OK].

*03* Select [File] - [Import] - [Import to Stage] or use the [Ctrl]-[R] shortcut.

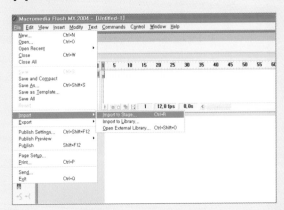

**04** Select the file **files\pdfSample.pdf** and click [Open].

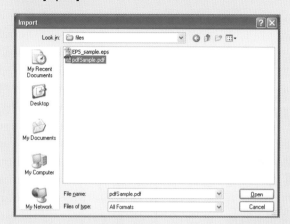

**05** In the Import Options dialog box, set [Convert pages to] to Scenes and click [OK].

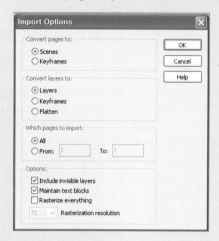

**06** Each of the pages within the PDF file will be loaded into the movie as a separate scene.

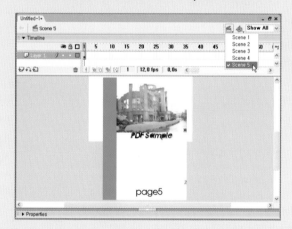

**Final File**
\Sample\Chapter06
\06_008_end.fla

**Import File**
\Sample\Chapter06\file
\EPS_sample.eps

# Loading EPS Files into Flash

**01** The image below shows the original file viewed with Adobe Photoshop.

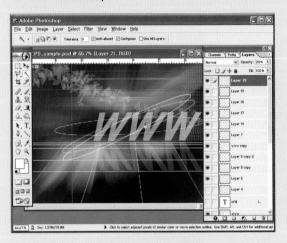

**02** Press [Ctrl]-[N] to open a new file, select [Flash Document], and click [OK].

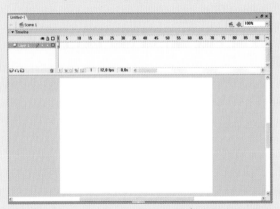

**03** Choose [File] - [Import] - [Import to Stage] or press [Ctrl]-[R].

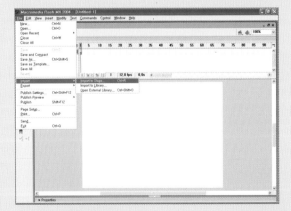

*04* Select the file **files\EPS_sample.eps** and click [Open].

*05* In the Import Options dialog box, set [Convert pages to] to Scenes and press [OK].

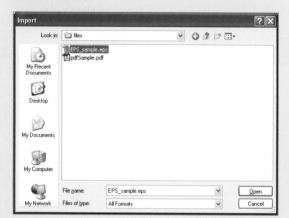

*06* The EPS file is loaded into Flash as five separate images stacked on top of one another. Drag the images to separate them as shown below.

Like PDF files, EPS (Encapsulated PostScript) files can be imported to Flash directly. This is convenient because it saves you the need to use a helper application to open or convert the file first. Keep this in mind during your projects as it will save you time if you can use existing files instead of starting from scratch.

Chapter | 7

# Working with Sounds

So far you have only learned to use Flash to create visual effects. In this chapter, you will learn to enhance your Flash movies by adding sound effects or even background music. There are many features within Flash that help you work with  sounds. However, adding sounds can also increase the size of a movie, so it is important to use them wisely.

# Adding Sounds in Flash

Flash supports several different types of sound files, including WAV and MP3. You can create your own files or download copyright-free sounds from the Internet. In this section, you will learn how to include sound files in a movie and explore some of the audio options available in Flash.

## Importing a Sound File

Like any other external file, sound is imported into Flash using the Import command. Select [File] - [Import] - [Import to Library], choose the sound you want to import, and press [OK]. The sound will then be added to the library.

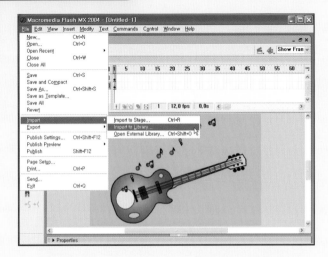

**tip >>**

If you have imported a sound file, you should see the name of the file as well as the word 'Sound' in the Kind column of the library.

## Inserting a Sound File Into a Movie

After you have imported a sound into the library, you must add it to the movie before it will play. You can do this either by dragging the sound from the library onto the stage, or by selecting it from the Property Inspector.

# Using the Library

To add a sound to your movie, select a keyframe and drag the sound from the library onto the stage. The sound will then be inserted into that keyframe. You can spot frames that contain sound by the blue waveform that appears.

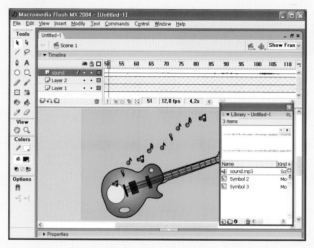

# Using the Property Inspector

You can also use the Property Inspector to add a sound to your movie. Select the keyframe and choose the name of the sound from the drop-down menu in the Property Inspector.

# Removing a Sound from the Timeline

You can stop a sound from playing in your movie by either using the Property Inspector or by clearing the keyframe containing the sound.

# Using the Property Inspector

To remove a sound using the Property Inspector, select the frame where the sound has been added and set the Sound name to None.

# Using the Clear Keyframe Command

You can clear a sound from a keyframe by right-clicking the keyframe and selecting [Clear Keyframe].

## Deleting a Sound File

Removing the sound from the timeline will not delete it from the library. You can delete the sound by selecting it in the library and clicking the trash can icon (🗑). Sounds and symbols deleted this way cannot be recovered using the Undo command.

Sound Property Inspector

## Sound Option Menu

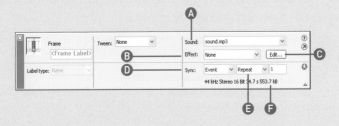

Ⓐ **Sound**: Sound files within the library.

Ⓑ **Effect**: Effects for sound files including fades and panning.

Ⓒ **Edit**: Opens the Edit Envelope dialog box. You can use this to edit effects or change volume levels.

Ⓓ **Sync**: Choose how the sound will be played within the movie.
   a. Event: An event sound plays when the movie reaches a keyframe. The sound keeps playing until finished.
   b. Start: The Start option plays the sound when the keyframe plays. If no Stop option is included, Start works in the same way as Event.
   c. Stop: Stops the sound immediately when a keyframe is reached.
   d. Stream: Sound will play as soon as the minimum amount of sound data has been transmitted, rather than waiting for the entire sound to load. The sound file is synchronized to the animation.

Ⓔ **Repeat/Loop**: Used to specify how many times the sound will loop or repeat. Looping is useful if you have a short sound file that is played throughout the movie.

Ⓕ Displays the information on the recording settings for the selected sound file.

# Using Behaviors to Control Sound

There are five behaviors that you can use to work with sound files in Flash. You can use these behaviors to load a sound from the library onto the stage, load and play a streaming MP3 file, play a sound file, stop a sound file, or stop all sounds.

Some of the behaviors require a linkage name or instance name so that you can use ActionScript. A linkage name is a little like an instance name, as it allows you to specify a name for a library symbol.

## Behaviors for Use with Sound Files

| Behavior | Explanation | Parameters |
|---|---|---|
| Load Sound from Library | Loads a sound from the library using the linkage ID. | Linkage ID in library sound instance name. |
| Load streaming MP3 file | Loads and plays a streaming MP3 file. | MP3 file name and path. |
| Play Sound | Plays a sound instance. | Sound instance name. |
| Stop All Sounds | Stops all sounds that are currently playing. | No parameters. |
| Stop Sound | Stops a sound instance. | Sound instance name. |

# 1 Adding Background Music

Background music can enhance the overall effect of a Flash movie. However, if you use an entire song as your background music it will greatly increase the file size of the movie. One way to overcome this problem is to use a small sound loop that plays over and over again. You can use a sound-editing program to create a loop or download a copyright-free sound loop from the Internet.

**Start File**
　\Sample\Chapter07\07_001.fla

**Final File**
　\Sample\Chapter07\07_001_end.fla

**Import File**
　\Sample\Chapter07\sound
　\sound2.mp3

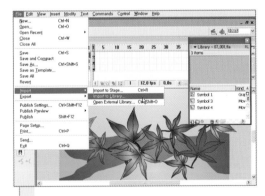

1 Open the start file and select [File] - [Import] - [Import to Library].

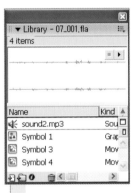

2 Select the **sound2.mp3** file and press [OK]. The file will be imported into the library.

3 Click frame 1 of the sound layer and select sound2.mp3 from the Sound drop-down in the Property Inspector. Under Sync options, change from Repeat to Loop.

4 Save the movie using the [Ctrl]-[S] shortcut. Press [Ctrl]-[Enter] to test the movie.

# Adding a Sound to a Button

Buttons are symbols that react to mouse actions. You can add sounds that play at various stages of a button being clicked–when the mouse is over the button, when the button is clicked, and when the mouse is away from the button. In this section, you will add sounds into each frame of the button timeline.

**Start File**

\Sample\Chapter07\07_002.fla

**Final File**

\Sample\Chapter07\07_002_end.fla

**Import Files**

\Sample\Chapter07\sound\bird.wav

\Sample\Chapter07\sound\bird2.wav

\Sample\Chapter07\sound\bird3.wav

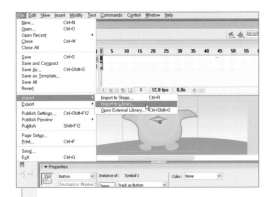

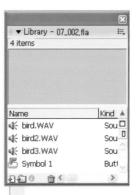

[1] Open the start file and select [File] - [Import] - [Import to Library].

[2] Select bird.wav, bird2.wav, and bird3.wav and click [Open].

[3] Press [Ctrl]-[L] to view the sounds in the library.

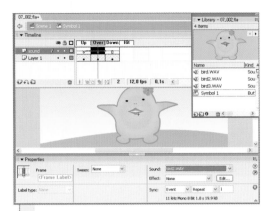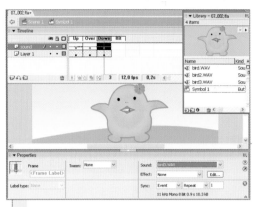

**4** Double-click the symbol1 button on the stage to enter Symbol Edit mode. Insert a layer above Layer 1 and name it **sound**. Insert keyframes in the Over and Down frames by pressing [F6].

**5** Select the Up frame and set the Sound to bird.wav in the Property Inspector. Set the Over frame to bird2.wav and the Down frame to bird3.wav.

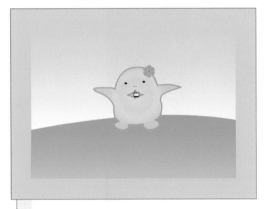

**6** Press [Ctrl]-[Enter] to test the movie. Click the buttons to check that the sounds play as you interact with the button.

# Using Sounds in an Animation

Sounds can be used in different ways within a movie–as background music, button effects, and even for adding sound effects into your animations. In this example, you will add sound effects and background music to a movie.

**Start File**
\Sample\Chapter07\07_003.fla

**Final File**
\Sample\Chapter07\07_003_end.fla

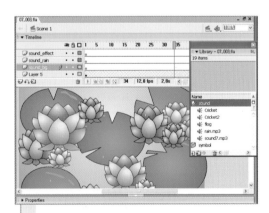

[1] Open the start file. Press [Ctrl]-[L] and open the sound folder in the Library.

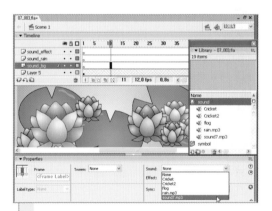

[2] Click a frame in the sound_bg layer. In the Property Inspector, set the Sound to sound7.mp3 and Sync to Start.

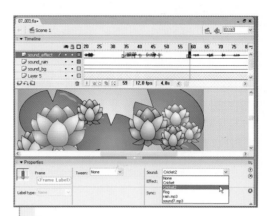

**3** Select the sound_rain layer. In the Property Inspector, set the Sound to rain.mp3, the Sync to Start, and change Repeat to Loop.

**4** Select the sound_effect layer and add keyframes at frames 15, 35, and 59 with the [F6] key.

**5** Click on frame 15 and set the Sound to Cricket in the Property Inspector. Select frame 35 and set the Sound to frog. In frame 59, set the Sound to Cricket2.

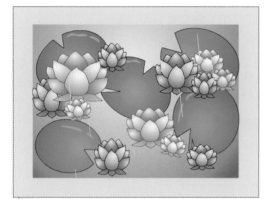

**6** Press [Ctrl]-[Enter] to test the movie.

# Turning off Sounds within a Movie

Although background music can enhance a movie, it is good idea to allow the user to turn off the music. In this example, you will add a toggle button that turns the sound on and off within the movie.

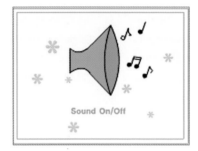

**Start File**

\Sample\Chapter07\07_004.fla

**Final File**

\Sample\Chapter07\07_004_end.fla

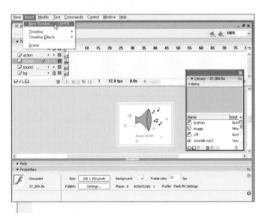

1 Open the start file and select [Insert] - [New Symbol].

**tip >>**

The shortcut keys to create a new symbol are [Ctrl]-[F8].

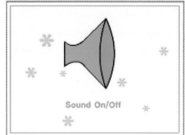

2 In the Create New Symbol dialog box, enter the name **sound**, set the behavior to Movie Clip, and click [OK]. You will be in Symbol Edit mode.

3 Click frame 1 and select sound6.mp3 from the Sound drop-down menu in the Property Inspector.

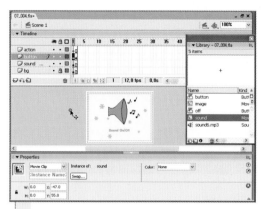

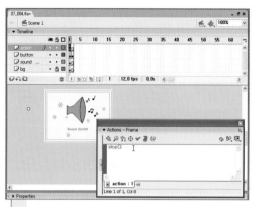

4 Return to the main stage and click frame 1 of the button layer. Drag the sound movie clip from the library onto the stage. It doesn't matter where you drag the sound movie clip as long as it appears somewhere on the stage.

5 Select frame 1 of the action layer and press [F9] to open the Actions panel. Remove the stop(); action.

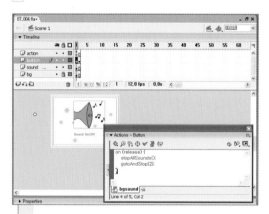

```
code
1 on(release) {
2     stopAllSounds();
3     gotoAndStop(2);
4 }
```

**Line 1**: Actions will be triggered by the onRelease event (i.e., releasing the mouse button).
**Line 2**: Stop all sounds currently playing in the movie.
**Line 3**: Go to frame 2 and stop playing.

6 Select the object in frame 1 of the button layer and enter the actions to the right in the Actions panel.

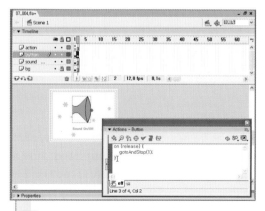

```
code
1 on(release) {
2     gotoAndStop(1);
3 }
```

**Line 1**: Actions will be triggered by the onRelease event (i.e., releasing the mouse button).
**Line 2**: Go to frame 1 and stop playing the movie.

7 Select the object in frame 2 of the button layer and enter the actions shown here in the Actions panel.

8 Press [Ctrl]-[Enter] to test the movie. Click the button to make sure that the sound plays and stops as expected.

# Making a Jukebox

You can add actions to buttons so that they will play and stop sounds within a movie. In this example, you will create a jukebox that allows users to select the sound they want to hear or to turn off all sound within the movie.

**Start File**
\Sample\Chapter07\07_005.fla

**Final File**
\Sample\Chapter07\07_005_end.fla

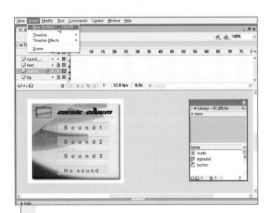

1 Open the start file and select [Insert] - [New [Symbol].

2 Set the name to **sound**, the behavior to Movie Clip, and click [OK].

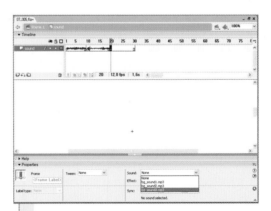

3 Insert keyframes at frames 1, 10, and 20 of the symbol. Change the name of Layer 1 to **sound**. Add bg_sound1.mp3 at frame 1, bg_sound2.mp3 at frame 10, and bg_sound3.mp3 at frame 20 using the Property Inspector. Use the [F5] key to extend the animation to 30 frames.

**4** Insert a layer above the sound layer and insert keyframes at frames 9, 19, and 30.

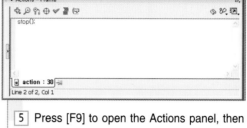

**5** Press [F9] to open the Actions panel, then enter a stop(); action in each keyframe.

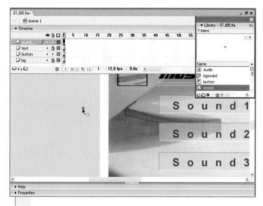

**6** Return to the main stage. Select the sound_mov layer and drag the sound movie clip onto the stage from the library.

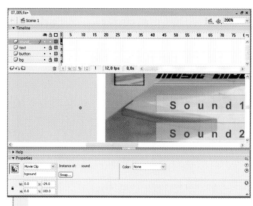

**7** Select the sound movie clip on the stage and enter **bgsound** for the instance name in the Property Inspector.

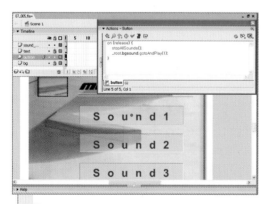

**8** Select the Sound 1 button on the button layer, open the Actions panel, and enter the actions shown here.

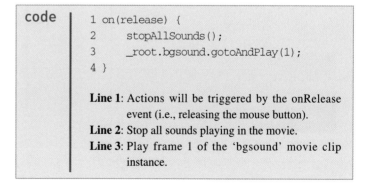

```
code
1 on(release) {
2     stopAllSounds();
3     _root.bgsound.gotoAndPlay(1);
4 }
```

**Line 1**: Actions will be triggered by the onRelease event (i.e., releasing the mouse button).
**Line 2**: Stop all sounds playing in the movie.
**Line 3**: Play frame 1 of the 'bgsound' movie clip instance.

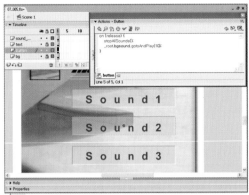

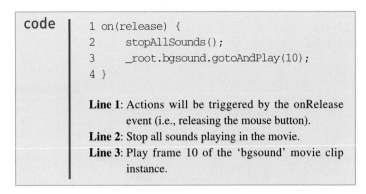

```
code   1 on(release) {
       2     stopAllSounds();
       3     _root.bgsound.gotoAndPlay(10);
       4 }
```

**Line 1**: Actions will be triggered by the onRelease event (i.e., releasing the mouse button).
**Line 2**: Stop all sounds playing in the movie.
**Line 3**: Play frame 10 of the 'bgsound' movie clip instance.

9 Select the Sound 2 button and enter the script shown here in the Actions panel.

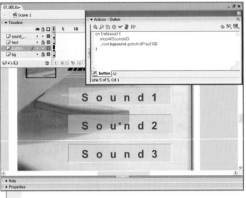

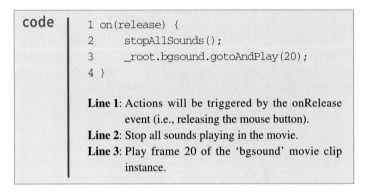

```
code   1 on(release) {
       2     stopAllSounds();
       3     _root.bgsound.gotoAndPlay(20);
       4 }
```

**Line 1**: Actions will be triggered by the onRelease event (i.e., releasing the mouse button).
**Line 2**: Stop all sounds playing in the movie.
**Line 3**: Play frame 20 of the 'bgsound' movie clip instance.

10 Select the Sound 3 button and enter the script shown here in the Actions panel.

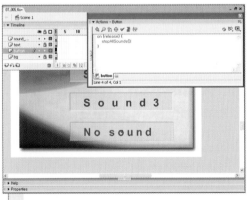

```
code   1 on(release) {
       2     stopAllSounds();
       3 }
```

**Line 1**: Actions will be triggered by the onRelease event (i.e., releasing the mouse button).
**Line 2**: Stop all sound playing in the movie.

11 Select the No sound button and enter the following in the Actions panel.

12 Press [Ctrl]-[Enter] to test the movie.

Behaviors can be used to work with either library sounds or external sound files. For example, you can use behaviors to play and stop external MP3 files in real time.

**Start File**
\Sample\Chapter07\07_006.fla

**Final File**
\Sample\Chapter07
\07_006_end.fla

**Import Files**
\Sample\Chapter07
\sound\sound1.mp3

\Sample\Chapter07
\sound\sound2.mp3

# Using Behaviors to Control Sound

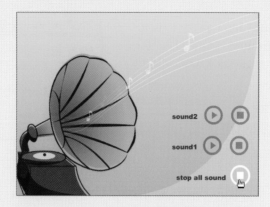

**01** Open the start file. It shows two sound names-sound1 and sound2-each with buttons for playing and stopping the sounds. There is also a button instance (stop all sound) that stops all sounds from playing.

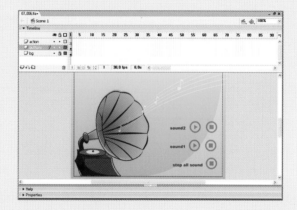

**02** Click the sound1 play button. From the Behaviors panel, choose [Sound] - [Load streaming MP3 file].

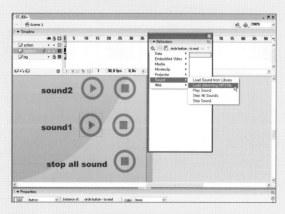

**03** Enter **sound/sound1.mp3** as the URL for the MP3 file to load. Enter **s1_sound** as the name for this sound instance. Click [OK].

**04** Click the sound1 stop button and add the [Sound] - [Stop Sound] behavior.

**05** Enter **s1_sound** as the name of the sound instance to stop. This will stop the external MP3 file from playing.

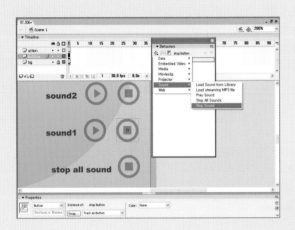

**06** Click the sound2 play button. Select [Sound] - [Load streaming MP3 file] from the Behaviors panel.

**07** Enter **sound/sound2.mp3** as the URL for the MP3 file to load. Enter **s2_sound** as the name for this sound instance. Click [OK].

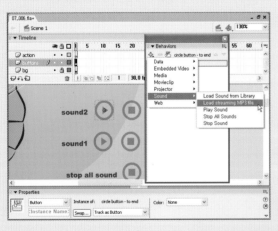

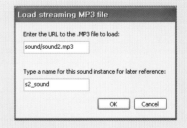

**08** Select the sound2 stop button. Choose [Sound] - [Stop Sound] from the Behaviors panel.

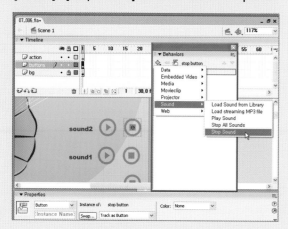

**09** Type **s2_sound** for the name of the sound instance to stop.

**10** The two Stop buttons will turn off sound1 and sound2 individually. The last button will stop any sound that is playing. Click the stop all sound button and choose [Sound] - [Stop All Sounds] from the Behaviors panel.

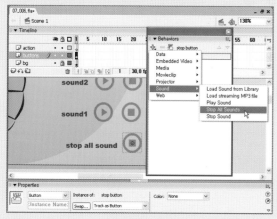

**11** Click [OK].

**12** Press [Ctrl]-[Enter] to test the movie. Click each of the buttons to see their effects.

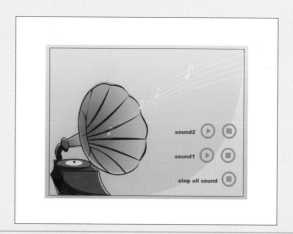

**Chapter** | 8

# It's a Wrap!

So far you've been previewing and testing your movies within Flash. Before you publish a movie, however, you'll need to optimize it by considering issues such as your audience, the final destination for your Flash movie, and the size and structure of your movie files. In this chapter, we will look at the things to consider when publishing your movies.

# From Optimization to the Final Cut

For a Flash movie to reach a wide audience over the Internet, it is important to keep the file size small. In this chapter, you will learn to optimize a movie, use the Bandwidth Profiler to check if the movie will load properly at different connection speeds, and lastly, to publish a Flash Player file and an optional HTML file.

## Optimizing Objects

The first thing to consider is the way that objects are used within the movie. If an object is used more than once, it should be registered as a symbol within the library. Symbols are loaded only once in each movie regardless of the number of times that they appear on the stage. Each symbol can have different settings such as size, color, and position on the stage.

You should also group your objects wherever possible, as it reduces the workload for the Flash Player.

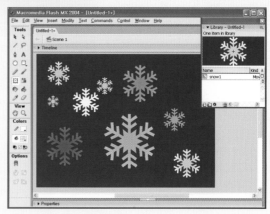

Reusing Symbols from the Library

## Optimizing Color

Gradients are more complicated to process than solid colors and require more space, so you should minimize the number of gradients that you use. Using alpha transparencies can also make your movie run more slowly. It is advisable to use brightness values instead of animating with alpha values where possible.

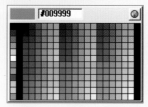

## Optimizing Lines

### Line Style

Your choice of line style can also affect the file size. Solid lines take up less memory than non-solid lines, as shown to the right.

A Comparison of Object File Sizes Using Different Line Styles

### Curves

1 You can also reduce file size by simplifying any vector images that you import into Flash. Firstly, break apart the image using [Ctrl]-[B] and optimize the curves within the shape using [Modify] - [Shape] - [Optimize].

2 The Optimize command reduces unnecessary curves from the image and can reduce the overall size of the file.

3 Bear in mind, however, that overusing the Optimize command can distort the original shape.

## Optimizing Text

### Small Fonts

Anti-aliasing softens the text edges and gives a smoother appearance to letters. However, small-sized fonts can become illegible when the text is anti-aliased. You can remove anti-aliasing from text by clicking the [Alias Text] icon () in the Property Inspector.

Activating the Alias Text Icon

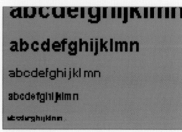

Aliased Text

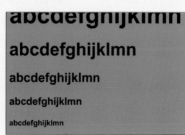

Anti-Aliased Text

## Fonts

When you use a font in your Flash movie, it is embedded within the SWF file. Using a large number of font faces and font styles can increase the size of your movie unnecessarily. You should also avoid breaking apart fonts unless necessary, as this will add to the movie size.

The Text 'Hello World!' is Shown in Different Fonts

## Optimizing Bitmap Images

Flash works best with vector images, so avoid using bitmaps unless they are necessary for your movie. Each time you include a bitmap image, you will increase the size of your movie by a relatively substantial margin.

You should avoid animating bitmaps, since Flash stores one copy of the image in each frame of the animation. If possible, trace the bitmap to convert it into a vector image.

Whenever you use a bitmap within Flash, it should be compressed.

## Compressing Individual Bitmap Images

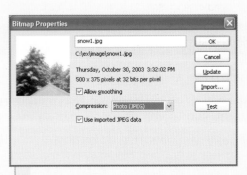

1  You can select the compression settings for an image by right-clicking the image in the library and selecting [Properties] in the shortcut menu.

2  In the Bitmap Properties dialog box, choose the type of compression that you want to apply from the [Compression] drop-down box.

tip >>

**Bitmap Image Compression Screen**

You can also access the Export Movie dialog box by selecting [File] - [Publish Settings] and clicking the [Flash] tab.

270

## Compressing All Bitmap Images

[1] You can compress bitmap images in the movie using the same settings all at once. Select [File] - [Export] - [Export Movie].

[2] In the Export Flash Player dialog box, use the slider to set the JPEG quality. As you decrease the value, both the file size and image quality will reduce.

## Optimizing Sound Files

Sound files can greatly increase the size of Flash movies. Using short sound loops for background music can help to minimize the file size. If you are sampling your own sounds, use the lowest bit depth and sample rate that gives you an acceptable quality.

Wherever possible, you should use MP3 files instead of WAV or other formats, as MP3s have a much higher compression rate. You can also compress sounds within Flash by changing compression settings for a single sound or for all sounds within the movie.

## Compressing Individual Sounds

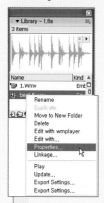

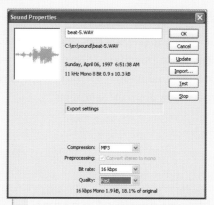

[1] You can compress a sound by right-clicking the sound file name in the library and selecting [Properties].

[2] In the Sound Properties dialog box, select the Compression settings. You can also change the Bit rate and Quality settings.

## Compressing All Sounds

1 You can apply the same sound compression settings to all sounds within a movie by selecting [File] - [Publish Settings]. Select the [Flash] tab and click the [Set] button to edit the Audio Stream and Audio Event options.

2 You can then make changes in the Sound Settings dialog box.

## Other Considerations

### Using Tweened Animations

Use tweened animations wherever possible, since they take up less file space than frame-by-frame animations. Limit the amount of motion that happens in each frame. Animating several objects at the same time or creating animations that contain large changes can affect the speed at which the movie runs.

### Limiting Modify Shape Commands

The [Convert Line to Fills], [Expand Fill], and [Soften Fill Edges] commands in the [Modify] - [Shape] drop-down menu should only be used where necessary, since they increase file size and slow down the animation.

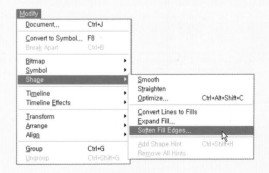

### Deleting Unnecessary Content

- All blank or unnecessary frames and keyframes
- Empty layers
- Unused objects inside layers

## Bandwidth Profiler

There are several ways to test how well your Flash movie loads before it is published. The Bandwidth Profiler helps you see how well your Flash movie has been optimized. It is useful in determining whether the movie will load properly at different Internet speeds.

If your movie is complex, you might want to stop the movie from playing until all of the frames in the movie have been loaded. This will ensure that playback is smooth. To keep the user's interest, you can create a preloader, which is a simple animation that plays while the user waits for the movie to download.

## Opening the Bandwidth Profiler

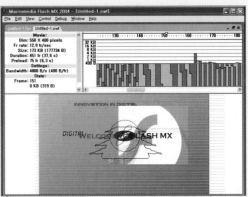

1 Test the movie with the [Ctrl]-[Enter] shortcut. Select [View] - [Bandwidth Profiler] from the Test Movie window.

2 The Bandwidth Profiler window opens.

## Bandwidth Profiler Graphs

The Bandwidth Profiler allows you to see two different types of graphs–the streaming graph and the frame-by-frame graph. The graphs show the file size of each frame. The red line in the middle of the graph shows the limits of the selected download speed. Areas above the red line are frames where the movie may have to pause to download before playing.

### Streaming Graph

Within Flash, the first part of the movie is downloaded and played while the rest of the frames are loaded in the background. The streaming graph shows the frames in which the loading takes place. Choose [View] - [Show Streaming] to toggle the streaming graph on and off.

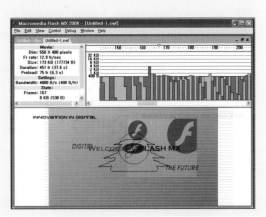

## Frame-By-Frame Graph

The frame-by-frame graph displays the size of each frame and is useful in determining which frames may cause the loading of the movie to slow down.

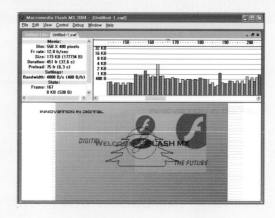

# Simulating Download Time

The speed of the Internet connection used to view a Flash movie played over the Web determines how smoothly the movie plays. It is important to identify the likely Internet connection speeds of your audience and tailor the movie accordingly.

You can simulate different download speeds to test how long it takes for the movie to be loaded for users with different Internet connections. Select [View]-[Download Settings] and choose a download speed. You can then watch the download at that speed by selecting [View] - [Simulate Download].

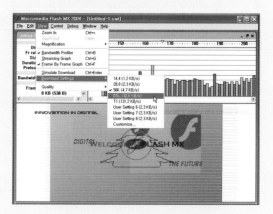

## The Bandwidth Profiler Window

Ⓐ **Dim**: Movie dimensions.

Ⓑ **Fr rate**: Frame rate in frames per second.

Ⓒ **Size**: Movie file size in KB.

Ⓓ **Duration**: Total number of frames and total length of movie.

Ⓔ **Preload**: How long it takes to load the movie with the current bandwidth.

Ⓕ **Bandwidth**: Number of bytes of data that are transmitted per frame.

Ⓖ **Frame**: Size of the selected frame number and object.

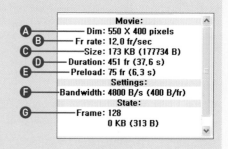

## Publishing a Movie

Each time you press [Ctrl]-[Enter] to test a movie, you create a SWF file. You can preview the file in Flash or double-click it to view it in the Flash Player. In this section, you'll look at publishing a movie so that it can be added to a Web site or CD-ROM.

Publishing a movie not only creates the SWF file but can also generate files such as an HTML page, a static image, a QuickTime movie, or a standalone Flash Projector file. Select [File] - [Publish] or use the shortcut keys [Shift]-[F12] to publish your files.

### Publish Settings Command

Publishing outputs the Flash movie in different file formats. You can decide how to publish the file by selecting [File] - [Publish Settings] and choosing options from the Publish Settings dialog box.

### Property Inspector

You can also access the Publish settings through the Property Inspector. Click outside the stage and the Property Inspector will display the document properties. Click the [Settings] button next to Publish to open the Publish Settings dialog box.

### Publishing Formats

The [Formats] tab of the Publish Settings dialog box allows you to choose the formats that you'd like use for your movie. Each time you check a format type checkbox, an extra tab will be added to the Publish Settings dialog box. The tab contains the publishing options for that file type.

When you publish the movie, each of the selected file types will be created.

Selecting File Types

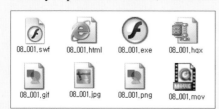

Created Files

# Creating Flash Player File Format (SWF)

- An SWF file is created every time you test a Flash movie.

- You can select [File] - [Export] - [Export Movie] to access the Export Movie dialog box. This allows you to export the movie in a number of different formats including SWF.

- An SWF file can also be created by selecting [File] - [Publish Settings] and checking the Flash (SWF) option. To view the Flash setup options, click the [Flash] tab in the Publish Settings dialog box.

## Flash Player Format (SWF) Publishing Settings

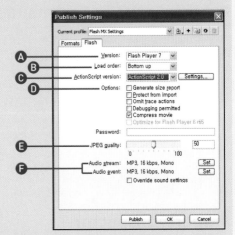

**Ⓐ Version**: Select a Flash Player version between Flash Player 1 and Flash Player 7.

**Ⓑ Load order**: Allows you to determine the order in which the layers of the first frame will be loaded.

> *Bottom up*: Loads from the bottom layer upwards.
>
> *Top down*: Loads from the top layer downwards.

**Ⓒ ActionScript version**: Choose between ActionScript 2.0 and ActionScript 1.0.

**Ⓓ Options**:

> *Generate size report*: Movie information is generated as a TXT file.
>
> *Protect from import*: Stop others from importing the SWF file into Flash.
>
> *Omit trace actions*: When the test movie is run, this option suppresses any ActionScript Trace actions.
>
> *Debugging permitted*: The published movie can be debugged.
>
> *Compress movie*: Always set on by default. This option compresses the SWF file and is available for Flash Player 6 and later versions.
>
> *Optimize for Flash Player 6 r65*: This option appears only when the Version is set to Flash Player 6. This is used to optimize Flash Player 6 r65.

**Ⓔ JPEG quality**: Used to compress bitmap images used in the movie with a compression setting between 0% and 100%.

**Ⓕ Audio stream and Audio event**: These options are used to set the compression for all Streaming and Event sounds in the movie. If [Override sound settings] is not checked, individual sound settings in the library will override the general settings.

## Generating HTML

The Publish feature can be used to generate an HTML page that displays the SWF file on a Web page. Select [File] - [Publish Settings] and check the HTML option. When you publish the movie, an HTML file will be created.

08_001.swf    08_001.html

The Published SWF and HTML Files

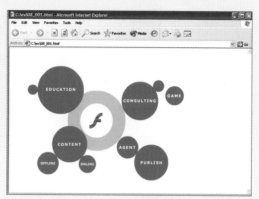

Displaying a Flash Movie in Internet Explorer

tip >>

### What Is HTML?

HTML, or Hyper Text Mark-Up Language, is the language used to write documents that are viewed in a Web browser. An HTML document is composed of a set of tags, and the Publish feature can generate the required HTML tags so you can display your SWF file on a Web page.

# Using Export Movie
# to Make an SWF File

When movies are published, the FLA file will be saved along with an SWF file of the same name. However, if you use the Export Movie command to create the movie, you can create an SWF file with a different name and save it in a different folder. The command can also create an SWF file without first having to save the FLA file.

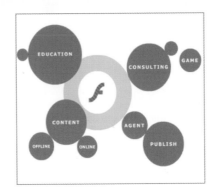

**Start File**

\Sample\Chapter08\08_001.fla

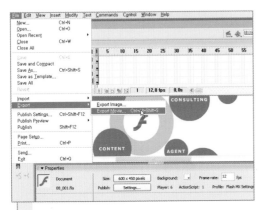

[1] Open the start file. Select [File] - [Export] - [Export Movie].

[2] In the Export Movie dialog box, type in **Solution** for the file name, and choose a save location for the file. Click [Save].

[3] In the Export Flash Player dialog box, accept the default properties for the SWF file and click [OK].

[4] The SWF file has been created. You can double-click the file to view it in the Flash Player.

# 2 Creating Full-Screen Movies for CD-ROMs

When creating Flash movies for CD-ROMs, two things are important. Firstly, the movies need to be created as EXE files so that they can be played on any PC, regardless of whether or not the Flash Player is installed. Secondly, most Flash movies made for CD-ROMs need to play in full-screen mode. In this example, you will learn how to make a full-screen EXE file that can be played on any PC.

**Start File**
> \Sample\Chapter08\08_002.fla

**Final File**
> \Sample\Chapter08\08_002_end.exe

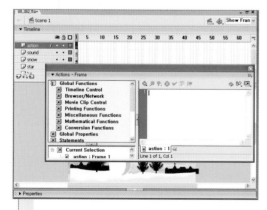

1 Open the start file and save it to your hard drive. Insert a layer and name it **action**. Press [F9] to open the Actions panel.

2 Select frame 1 of the action layer and click [Global Functions] - [Browser/Network]. Double-click [fscommand] and type "fullscreen", "true" inside the brackets.

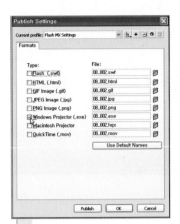

3 Select [File] - [Publish Settings].

4 Check [Windows Projector] (.exe) in the [Format] tab. Click the [Publish] button and then press [OK].

5 You will see that an EXE file has been created in the folder where the original Flash movie was saved. Double-click the EXE file to open it as a Windows Projector file.

6 You should see the full-screen movie above. Press [Esc] to return the movie to its original size.

# 3

# Creating Transparent Flash Movies

In this example we'll publish a Flash movie with a transparent background. The movie will automatically adopt the background color of the Web page upon which it's viewed.

**Start File**
\Sample\Chapter08\08_003.fla

**Final File**
\Sample\Chapter08 \08_003_01_end.html

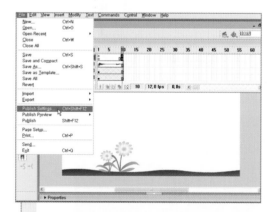

1 Open the start file and save it to your hard drive. Select [File] - [Publish Settings].

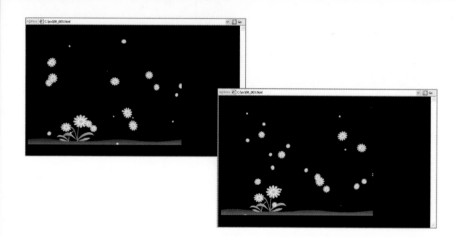

2 Make sure the HTML file type is checked and select the [HTML] tab. Click the [Window Mode] drop-down menu and select Transparent Windowless. Press the [Publish] button at the bottom and then click [OK].

3 You should see that an HTML document has been created in the folder where the original Flash movie was saved. Double-click the HTML file.

tip >>

## Inserting Flash Movies into Dreamweaver

If you want to insert a transparent Flash file into Dreamweaver, you don't need to create the HTML page using Flash. Instead, include the code wmode = "transparent", with the Flash file to be inserted.

4 A Web browser window will open. If you are using Internet Explorer, choose [View] - [Source] to see the HTML code.

5 The HTML source contains the line wmode = "transparent". This is the HTML code that makes the movie transparent.

6 To check that the movie is transparent, change the line <body bgcolor="#ffffff"> to read <body bgcolor="#000000">.

7 Select [File] - [Save] to save the HTML file.

8 Click the [Refresh] button of your browser. You will see that the background color has changed to black and that the Flash movie is transparent.

### Let`s Go Pro!

# Matching the Flash Movie Size to the Window Size

When you create a Flash movie, you can set the height and width of the stage. In this exercise, you will set the movie up to automatically match the size of the window in which it is shown.

**Start File**
\Sample\Chapter08\08_003.fla

**Final File**
\Sample\Chapter08
\08_003_02_end.html

*01* Open the start file and select [File] - [Publish Settings].

*02* Click the [HTML] tab and choose Percent from the [Dimensions] drop down-menu. Make sure that the scale is set to Default (Show all). Press the [Publish] button and then click [OK].

*03* Double-click the HTML file that has been created and change the size of your browser window. You will see that the movie changes to the size of the browser window.

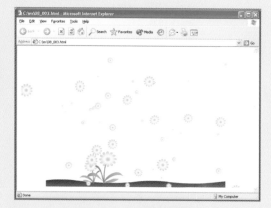

# Index >>>